W9-CJT-045

HURON COUNTY LIBRARY

2 008 137965 1

Wilfrid Laurier
The Great Conciliator

BARBARA ROBERTSON

PUBLIC LIBRARY STAFORTH

Toronto
OXFORD UNIVERSITY PRESS
1971

© Oxford University Press (Canadian Branch) 1971

ISBN 0—19—540192—1

1 2 3 4 5 6 — 6 5 4 3 2 1

Printed in Canada by John Deyell Limited

125595

Contents

JAN. 1 8 1972

Illustrations

All illustrations are reproduced by courtesy
of the Public Archives of Canada

1

Beginnings

Wilfrid Laurier was born in 1841 in St Lin, Canada East (Quebec). In 1896 he became the first French-Canadian Prime Minister of Canada and remained in that post for the next fifteen years—a golden period in Canada's history, for the country prospered as it had not done for half a century. He was in politics for twenty-two years before the Liberal victory of 1896, the last nine of them as leader of the opposition in parliament; and after 1911 he was leader of the Liberal opposition again until his death in 1919. As Prime Minister, Laurier seemed entirely at home with success, yet he was well acquainted with opposition and defeat. But he accepted both success and failure philosophically.

Laurier's main interest lay in getting English-speaking and French-speaking Canadians to live amicably together, a task beyond the powers of any individual but one at which Laurier worked longer and harder and came within closer reach of success than any other Canadian. He was not a subterranean person like his successor, Mackenzie King. He brought the issues that divided French and English out into the open, discussed them, and proposed the most rational solutions he could devise. His solutions were usually good, and since he was a brilliant speaker, he very nearly charmed the birds out of the trees. All the same, Laurier did not solve the problems of English-French relations; he simply dealt with them as they occurred in his time. The problems remain.

Laurier was named Wilfrid after the hero of Sir Walter Scott's novel *Ivanhoe*. Wilfrid of Ivanhoe lived in medieval England where, according to Scott, arrogant Norman conquerors dominated the sullen Saxons. His hero was Richard the Lionheart, who wanted to be an English, not a Norman, king; both wanted to escape from the dreary circle of Norman-Saxon hatreds into a larger English patriotism. The young French-Canadian Wilfrid was like the Saxon Wilfrid, for his people had been conquered. Three quarters of a century after the British conquest—only four years before Laurier was born—a good many French Canadians had followed their great *Patriote* leader, Louis-Joseph Papineau, in a rebellion against British rule. The Rebellion of 1837, half-hearted and mismanaged, was crushed by British forces; its French-Canadian leaders scattered in exile. The air was still black with defeat when Laurier was born in 1841, yet his family did not train him to nourish hatreds or harbour resentments. He grew quite naturally toward his future career as a statesman who wanted his countrymen to be Canadians first, English and French second.

In St Lin the villagers had heard the British guns in St Eustache in 1837; they had seen the town burning, though it was twenty miles away. But life went on—even after the imperial government decided in 1839 that to prevent any more rebellions French Canadians ought to be gently but firmly made over into English citizens. The imperial government was a long way off, however. St Lin was a little frontier village that stood on the gently rolling plains just south of the Laurentian highlands and beside the serenely flowing River

Achigan, which was often full of logs, for people were busy selling timber and turning the woods into farms.

Laurier's family, like those of all other French Canadians, was deep-rooted in Canada. His first Canadian ancestor was one of the soldiers who accompanied the deeply religious Maisonneuve and Jeanne Mance when they founded Montreal as a Christian mission in 1642; nine years later he was killed by an Iroquois tomahawk. But his heirs lived on. Eight generations later Wilfrid Laurier was born just twenty-five miles from the place where his ancestor had landed.

Laurier's grandfather and father were both farmers and surveyors. In this area where new farms were being laid out, surveying was a necessary profession. It was essential to get the boundaries of a farm surveyed in order to prevent endless arguments and expensive lawsuits with neighbours over who owned what. Laurier's grandfather Charles invented the "landlog", a machine that measured distances when attached to the wheel of a calèche. He succeeded in getting the Assembly of Quebec to grant him a patent, but failed to get any financial help for his experiments in measuring distances on land and sea. So his ingenuity had no practical results.

Laurier's father Carolus was popular both in his own French community and in the nearby Scottish settlements. He was a progressive man. In politics he was a *Patriote* who believed that Canadians ought to be governed by Canadians, not by Great Britain or by a local clique of English; as a farmer he was first in the neighbourhood to use a threshing machine instead of a flail for the harvest.

Wilfrid Laurier felt especially drawn to his mother, Marie Marcelle Martineau. She was intellectual and artistic, fond of books and drawing. On her side of the family Wilfrid was related to his contemporary, the eloquent young Quebec poet, Louis Fréchette. His mother lived forever in his memory, yet he was only seven years old when she died of tuberculosis in 1848. His sister Malvina died of the same disease in 1855 when she was just eleven, and weak lungs threatened Wilfrid Laurier for many years. Tuberculosis was called the "White Death" in Quebec and it ravaged whole families, who lived, like the Lauriers, in small rooms overheated by wood stoves. Laurier escaped with nothing worse than chronic bronchitis.

Carolus Laurier married again. Wilfrid's stepmother was Adeline Ethier, who had looked after his mother in her sickness. She proved a kind nurse and protector both to himself and to his sister while she lived. There were children by this second marriage, yet Laurier and his stepmother remained closely attached. He was fond of her always and visited her in St Lin right up to her death in 1904.

The education of Wilfrid Laurier did not run quite true to form for a French-Canadian boy. It began typically enough at the elementary school in the village. But his strongminded grandfather and father, who were ambitious for Wilfrid, were determined that he should have an English education. Wilfrid's stepmother and the local curé were not enthusiastic about this plan; nonetheless young Wilfrid, not quite eleven years old, was sent to New Glasgow, an hour's calèche drive away, where he was to live and go to school for the next two years. He was to have stayed with an Irish Roman Catholic family, the Kirks; but since there was illness in that family he lived for some months with another friend of his father's, John Murray, a Presbyterian storekeeper from whom Wilfrid acquired a slight Scottish accent. Murray offered to excuse the Catholic boy from the family prayers each evening, but Wilfrid decided to attend and grew to love the King James

version of the Bible—he was to read it all his life. From the
schoolmaster, Sandy MacLean, armed with a glass of Scotch
whisky and a leather strap, he learned to love English poetry
—Milton, Shakespeare, and Burns.

Wilfrid used to clerk at John Murray's store and practise
his English. He continued to do this when he left the Murrays
for the Kirks, where he found another happy home. Forty
years later Carolus Laurier wrote to his son: "Nancy Kirk
writes that her father is now over a hundred and beginning to
wander in his mind: 'he does not see us at all, but talks of
Wilfrid and of Ireland.' "

Wilfrid's formal education began in 1854 when he left New
Glasgow and entered the classical college at L'Assomption.
One of a few colleges that educated the élite of each generation—those young men who would become lawyers and
doctors and notaries and priests—it was not much older than
he was, for it had been founded only in 1832. The classical
colleges went further than an English high school, and ordinary students did not get to them—they were lucky to receive
an elementary education.

Life at the Church-run college was austere. The day began
for the boys at 5:25 a.m. and ended at eight in the evening;
in between there was very little time for anything but work.
There was a half-holiday on Thursday afternoons, and if the
weather was fine the boys could go to the woods. "All week
our main preoccupation was as to whether it would be fine
next Thursday," said Laurier to the boys at L'Assomption in
1883. On Wednesday evening they always sang with fervour
one particular line of the canticle: "Grant us a good day".

Most of the time was spent learning Latin—the very centre
of the course of studies—a little Greek, a great deal of
classical French literature, a little English, and some philos-

ophy, history, and mathematics. All his life Laurier was to keep his knowledge of, and fondness for, the Latin classics. His biographer, O.D. Skelton, remembered that "many a time in later years, when leaving for a brief holiday, Mr Laurier would slip into his bag a volume of Horace or Catullus or an oration of Cicero and, what is less usual, would read it." His love of Latin he acquired from the teacher-priests. Their conservatism, however, was harder to transfer. Laurier was one of the founders of a debating society at his college. When he once argued with too-great eloquence that "in the interests of Canada the French kings should have permitted the Huguenots to settle here", not only the debate but the debating society itself was concluded.

A fellow classmate, Arthur Dansereau, recalled in later years how popular Wilfrid was—he was "the pupil with the greatest following and the most influence". He was no athlete, for his frail health kept him from playing games. His popularity was almost certainly the result of his personality and intellect: already he combined a sweet nature with a very lively and independent mind. The priests also recognized his abilities and admired them. As for Laurier, he remembered L'Assomption with fondness all his life.

L'Assomption was followed in 1861 by McGill, the only university in Quebec where a student could learn English as well as French law. It is doubtful that McGill had a profound effect on Laurier, for he was older now and did not live at the university but merely attended its lectures for two hours a day. Much of his time was spent working as a clerk in the law office of Rodolphe LaFlamme.

After he came to Montreal, Laurier lived at the house of Dr Séraphin Gauthier, whose wife had known Wilfrid's mother years before in St Lin. The hospitable Gauthiers made the young student welcome, and though at first Laurier was a little shy and preoccupied, he soon ventured to join them and their large circle of friends for evenings of music and talk. Among the other members of the household were a Mme Lafontaine and her daughter Zoë. Mme Lafontaine was seriously ill, and Zoë divided her time between looking after her mother and giving piano lessons to support them both. It was soon obvious that young Laurier was much attracted to her. Indeed, the attraction was mutual, but the prospect of a romance was pretty dim. Her mother was dying; he had poor health and no money.

Wilfrid did well in his law courses at McGill and graduated in 1864, second in a class of eleven. His thesis was on constitutional law. As it won the highest mark, he was invited to give the valedictory address—in French.

The graduating class bade its farewell to the university in William Molson Hall, and Wilfrid gave his address before a large audience. He was tall—a little over six feet—and handsome of face, and he wore, probably for the last time on a platform, the rough, awkward-looking clothes of a country youth. (He always admired elegance of dress.) He described the role of the lawyer in the nation and then touched on a concern that was to dominate his life: "Two races share today the soil of Canada," he said. These races had not always been friends. "But I hasten to say it, and I say it to our glory, that race hatreds are finished on our Canadian soil. There is no longer any family here but the human family. It matters not the language people speak, or the altars at which they kneel." Lawyers, he thought, had a large role in bringing about this reconciliation, and a large duty to maintain "the union between the peoples, the secret of the future".

It may seem astonishing that Laurier could say in 1864—

even in a valedictory address, which is expected to be optimistic—that "race hatreds are finished on our Canadian soil". Only twenty-five years earlier, Lord Durham, sent to Canada by the imperial government to explore the causes of the rebellions of 1837, had found "two nations warring in the bosom of a single state". In 1841 Lower Canada and Upper Canada were united, against the will of the French Canadians and without their consent. Since then much had changed. A main object of the union was to destroy French-Canadian nationality, yet in less than ten years that object had been abandoned and French Canadians were enjoying a degree of self-government far beyond their previous experience. This astonishing recovery was largely the work of Louis-Hippolyte LaFontaine, who became in the difficult and confused days after 1841 the chief political leader of the French Canadians. He convinced his fellow citizens that they could best secure their own national survival by co-operation with the Reform party of Canada West (Ontario), led by Robert Baldwin. When the parties that LaFontaine and Baldwin led finally won a majority of seats in the legislature, these two leaders were invited to form the government by the Governor-General, Lord Elgin. The French-Canadian professional class, so numerous and so under-employed, was now able to share in the government of Canada—as clerks, school commissioners, magistrates, justices of the peace—and so it came to belong to them as it never had before.

To this new political involvement was added economic prosperity. Canals were finished, and in the 1850s railway building forged ahead, welcomed always by little towns dreaming of great futures. Trees fell in unprecedented numbers and lumber mills flourished. Americans and British both began to devour Canadian wheat, and its production doubled between 1851 and 1861. Most of the wheat came from Canada West, but even in Canada East the farmers were now better off, for they sold livestock and dairy products to the lumbermen and to the Americans across the border.

The 1850s were good years for French Canadians. Everyone ought to have been perfectly happy in the midst of this prosperity, but of course everyone was not. The prince of malcontents was Papineau, still first in the hearts of his countrymen but no longer their leader. He despised LaFontaine's policy of co-operation with the Reformers of Canada West and thought his victories hollow: as long as there was union with Canada West, there could never be any triumph for French-Canadian nationality. French Canadians listened with pleasure to Papineau but they voted for LaFontaine's men. LaFontaine, without any of Papineau's magnetic appeal, had made it clear to his fellow citizens that their nationality would be safe and their future prosperous if they remained united with Canada West.

Though LaFontaine won a large majority of votes, Papineau won a group of ardent young supporters, like him "the enemy of kings, nobles and priests", who were ready to devote their lives to winning liberty and national existence for French Canadians. They detested the seigniorial tenures and the priests' tithes; they thought education should be state-controlled, not directed by the clergy as it traditionally was. And above all they thought French Canadians would be freer cut loose from the British connection and joined to the United States: republics were better than monarchies.

Papineau's young followers, the *Rouges*, did not win much support from the French-Canadian community and they received the undying hostility of the Roman Catholic Church in Quebec. In particular they were opposed by the energetic

Bishop Bourget who detested the "Red Republicans" in France and wanted none of them in Canada. Bourget was an ultramontane Catholic. The term "ultramontane" first came to be used in medieval France and referred to those ardent Catholics who looked "beyond the mountains" to Rome as their final authority and opposed those who wanted to build up a national church. Ultramontanes thought that the authority of the Church was, and ought to be kept, superior to that of governments. Indeed, since the Church was the supreme authority on all moral questions, the government ought to be guided by it. Bourget detested the *Rouges*, who wanted to increase the powers of government at the expense of the Church. Ultramontanism grew in Quebec in the generation after 1848, but it wasn't only the ultramontanes who disliked the *Rouges* when they attacked the Church's tithe and its control of education. Many of the clergy began to oppose the *Rouges*; their support swung to LaFontaine's party and stayed there. It helped to keep not only LaFontaine in power but his successor, George Etienne Cartier, as well.

The buoyant and self-assured Cartier and the cool and reserved LaFontaine had similar political views. Both thought French Canadians could prosper in a united Canada if they allied themselves with sympathetic Upper Canadians and co-operated on matters of common interest. In Cartier's time that meant building railways, and Cartier was able to add the support of big business to that of the Church and to satisfy the majority of French Canadians that his party best ensured their survival and prosperity. Cartier had once been a follower of Papineau—he had actually fought on the *Patriote* side in 1837—but his radical days were over and the party he led became steadily more conservative. Its members came to be called *Bleus.*

As French Canadians became steadily more satisfied in United Canada—even the *Rouges* stopped promoting annexation with the United States—the English-speaking peoples of Canada West grew more frustrated. From the early 1850s they were in a majority in Canada, and yet they sent exactly the same number of representatives to the legislature of United Canada as Canada East. Worse still, it was the French-speaking members of Canada East who helped establish a separate-school system in Canada West when the majority of that section wanted a non-denominational school system. Further, a great many people in Canada West supported expansion into the Hudson's Bay Company territories in the West, which they believed the Americans were eyeing covetously. The French-speaking people of Canada East were not at all enthusiastic about such an enlargement of English-speaking influence. The legislature of United Canada came to reflect widespread indignation in Canada West. Soon it was impossible for even a skilful politician like John A. Macdonald to get much support for a policy of co-operation with his French-Canadian fellow Conservatives, the *Bleus* led by George Etienne Cartier. And the leading Liberal of Canada West, George Brown, did not get much support from the politicians of Canada East because his fellow Liberals there, the *Rouges*, were perennially in a minority. The consequence was deadlock: no political leader or combination of political leaders could get enough support in both Canada East and West to form a government, and by 1864 most had tried. In June nearly all the major Canadian politicians gratefully turned to the idea of Confederation as a solution to their problems. Under Confederation, all the British North American colonies would be united in one federal government, yet retain a little of their separate colonial existence as provinces

responsible for local matters. Canada West had the most to
gain, for by Confederation the unhappy union with Canada
East would be ended, and, it was hoped, expansion into the
Hudson's Bay Company territories would be facilitated. Canada East, largely satisfied with the union, had much less
reason to be enthusiastic, but all the same Cartier supported
Confederation: he was a realist who saw that the frustrations
of Canada West had to be dealt with.

The years after 1864 were exciting ones for a young *Rouge*
in Montreal. The *Rouges* were opposed to Cartier and Confederation on the one hand and Bourget and the authority of
the Church on the other. Laurier was young, but he was more
than a spectator in these struggles, for he himself was a
Rouge and a friend of *Rouges*. For a time he was a law
partner of Médéric Lanctôt, who fought ardently against
Confederation in his paper, *L'Union Nationale*, and in the
secret anti-Confederation society, Club Saint-Jean Baptiste.
Lanctôt was an enthusiast—about both causes and people—
and one of his enthusiasms was Laurier. After introducing
Laurier to a friend one day, he observed with characteristic
warmth (when Laurier had gone): "*There* is a head for you!
Did you notice it? The young man who has it on his shoul-
ders is sure to make himself heard of yet in the world. Why,
sir, he is a poet, an orator, a philosopher, a jurist—I cannot
pretend to enumerate all his talents; but mark my words, he
is a coming man. Do not forget that face."

It is not quite clear whether Laurier shared all of Lanctôt's
views about Confederation, though certainly he did not have
Lanctôt's ardent temperament; mostly he saw to the office
work, which Lanctôt neglected in favour of his higher causes.
Laurier was really much more like the *Rouge* leader, A.-A.
Dorion, who was moderate in temperament and politics,

though undeniably liberal. Dorion saw the necessity of appeasing the dissatisfied people of Canada West but he thought it should be done without endangering French-Canadian nationality. He opposed Confederation for any number of reasons: he thought it a much less democratic plan than the American constitution, and he thought it very wrong to make so radical a change without an election.

The most damaging weapon in the *Rouges'* armoury of complaints against Confederation was their insistence that Confederation would endanger French-Canadian nationality. French Canadians had equal power in the government of United Canada; in the new and larger Canada they would become a minority in an English-speaking country. Cartier argued that the cultural rights of French-Canadians would be assured within the province of Quebec, where the French would be a majority; but the *Rouges* pointed out that the central government could disallow any provincial legislation it chose. The *Rouges* played upon very real anxieties. Confederation was a leap in the dark for French Canadians, not all of whom were as naturally cheerful as Cartier. All the same, Cartier did remain in control: there was no election.

The *Rouges* might worry about French-Canadian survival in the new Confederation; a more immediate problem was *Rouge* survival. Their challenge did not come from English-speaking Canadians but from right at home—from the ultra-montane Bishop Bourget of Montreal. Bourget's particular target was the Institut Canadien in his diocese of Montreal. A number of Instituts Canadiens had been established in Canada East from the 1840s on; they served as libraries—there were no public libraries at the time—and gathering places for debates and lectures. The Institute in Montreal was by far the largest—in 1857 it had 700 members, some of them Protestant—and was very much a place where free speech and free thought were celebrated. It seemed a dangerous and revolutionary organization to Bishop Bourget, and it challenged the authority of the Church—for what was it supposed to be advocating freedom from if not the guidance of the Church?

Laurier became a member of the Institut Canadien soon after he came to Montreal in 1861. In 1865 and again the following year he was vice-president. In 1863 he had been one of a committee that attempted vainly to work out a compromise with Bishop Bourget over the "dangerous and immoral" books in the Institute's library. Later the Institute's members appealed to Rome against Bourget's severity; but the response was scarcely encouraging. The Institute's yearbooks for 1868 and 1869 were placed on the Index, the list of books Roman Catholics were forbidden to read. Bourget then forbade membership in the Institute to Catholics— that is, Catholic members would be deprived of Church sacraments. Under Bourget's attacks the Institute eventually died, though not without some spirited death struggles.

The contention between the Institute and the bishop reached its climax over the death of Joseph Guibord, a printer by trade. Guibord died in 1869 while he was still a member of the Institut Canadien, and his widow was refused an ecclesiastical burial for him in the Côte des Neiges cemetery. The more ardent *Rouges* now transferred their struggle with Bourget to the lawcourts. (One of the defence lawyers in the Guibord case was Laurier's former employer, Rodolphe LaFlamme.) The *Rouge* lawyers battled from lower to higher court to the highest of Canadian courts, the Judicial Committee of the Privy Council in Great Britain, where they were victorious: the Judicial Committee decided that Guibord did have a right to an ecclesiastical burial.

In September 1875 angry mobs and a locked cemetery made it impossible to carry out the court's decision; two months later Guibord was at last buried in the ecclesiastical part of the Côte des Neiges but without any church rites. The coffin was covered with cement and sheets of tin and scrap iron to make certain Guibord's resting place was secure, and troops came to keep order. The *Rouges* seemed to have won a triumph in the courts, but Bishop Bourget had the last word. He declared that "the place where the body of this rebellious child of the Church would be deposited should be made separate from the rest of the consecrated cemetery, so that it would only be a profane place."

Laurier left Montreal long before the final burial of Joseph Guibord, even before the Institute's yearbooks had been put on the Index. His departure was caused by his health, not Bishop Bourget. His lifelong friend, L.-O. David, later recalled: "I seem to see Laurier as he was then, ill and sad, grave and indifferent to all the turmoil raised around him. He passed through the midst of it like a shadow and seemed to say to us, 'Brother, we must all die.' " He collapsed in his office in the fall of 1866, coughing blood, and it seemed that he had little future to look forward to. His kind *Rouge* friends did the best they could for him. A.-A. Dorion, grieving at the death of his brother Eric, suggested that Laurier move to L'Avenir, one of the new French settlements in the Eastern Townships, where he could edit Eric Dorion's paper, *Le Défricheur*. There he could also practise law and, with luck, recover his health.

Before the end of 1866 Laurier had left Montreal, the Institut Canadien, and Bishop Bourget. He also left Zoë with nothing settled between them—and with another suitor, Pierre Valois, in the wings.

2
Member of Parliament

When the first issue of *Le Défricheur* was published in L'Avenir under Laurier's editorship on November 28, 1866, *Le Pays* of Montreal paid tribute to the new editor as a brilliant young man and looked forward to his "glorious career". Nevertheless Laurier soon became discouraged, for L'Avenir was badly named: it seemed to have no future. By the beginning of January, Laurier had moved again, this time to a pleasant town nearby called Arthabaskaville, the judicial centre of the county, set at the edge of rolling hills and heavy forests. He boarded in the home of Dr Poisson.

Le Défricheur moved with him and the weekly issues continued to appear, even though Laurier's interest in editing it was fast declining. For a short time it seemed to be an effective medium for the expression of *Rouge* opinions, particularly on the subject of Confederation. The federal union, Laurier said in the ringing tones so characteristic of the late Eric Dorion, would be "the tomb of the French race and the ruin of Lower Canada". This, however, was not the view of the people of Arthabaska, or even of Antoine-Aimée Dorion and other *Rouges* who were preparing to accept Confederation. After all, the British North America Act was likely to be passed and they would have no choice but to make the best of it. Laurier gave up his attacks.

The future of *Le Défricheur* became doubtful when, on top of Laurier's lack of interest, it received the hostile attention of Bishop LaFlèche, in whose diocese it was published, and the curés of the countryside, who spoke out strongly against it. Everything went steadily downhill—the paper's revenue, the weather, and Laurier's health. Subscribers and advertisers melted away, the winter entered its last and worst phase, and Laurier began to haemorrhage. On March 28 a paid notice appeared in the rival *Bleu* paper announcing that "Mr Laurier, suffering for a long time from a malady of the lungs which has suddenly come to assume alarming proportions, finds it necessary to interrupt for some time the publication of *Le Défricheur*."

Laurier's sickness and convalescence lasted well into June. When his health was more or less restored it was not to journalism that his thoughts turned but to the practice of law. He entered into a partnership with a *Bleu* lawyer, Eugène Crépeau, and in the litigious neighbourhood of Arthabaska his practice flourished in a modest rural way.

Laurier, who had been corresponding with Zoë, heard in January that she had become engaged to Pierre Valois. On May 12 he received a telegram from Dr Gauthier asking him to come to Montreal at once on an urgent matter. His first impulse was not to go, but he changed his mind and left for Montreal early the next morning.

It seems that Zoë was unhappy. She confessed to Dr Gauthier that it was Wilfrid whom she loved and the doctor decided to take matters into his own hands: thus the telegram. The first thing he did after Wilfrid arrived was to give him a thorough physical. Gauthier informed him that he had—might always have—chronic bronchitis, not consumption, but that he was otherwise in good shape. He also told an

Zoë Laurier, 1878

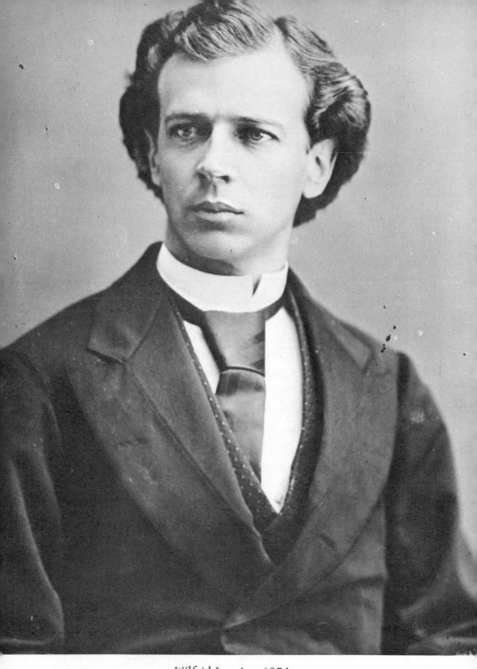

Wilfrid Laurier, 1874

unconvinced Laurier that he should marry, that Zoë wanted
him. When the two young people came face to face, in the
library of Gauthier's house, their doubts and hesitations
vanished. The marriage contract was drawn up that very
afternoon and Wilfrid and Zoë were married in the evening,
at eight o'clock. They returned to the house after the ceremony to meet an incredulous Pierre Valois, who recovered
from his shock and stayed to toast the bride.

That same evening the Lauriers parted. Wilfrid had to
return to Arthabaska for a court case, but Zoë was not ready
to leave home on such short notice. She soon followed,
however.

Fifty years later Laurier recalled the idyllic period that
immediately followed his marriage. "Those days of Arthabaska, so faint, so remote that they seem almost a dream. We
were young then, and youth paints only *en couleur de rose*.
Those days of Arthabaska! How gladly I would return to
them." Wilfrid and Zoë lived in three rooms of Dr Poisson's
home, one of which was made into a study for Wilfrid. They
made a great many friends in a neighbourhood that was
enlivened by artists, musicians, and poets.

Laurier occupied himself with his work and his reading. He
read widely, in French and English literature and in history.
His interests ranged from the French-Canadian historian
François-Xavier Garneau through the classics of French literature—Bossuet, Molière, and on to the romantics like Victor
Hugo. In English his favourite authors were Shakespeare,
Macaulay, and the Manchester radical, John Bright. He was
particularly interested in Bright's American friend, Abraham
Lincoln; he collected Lincoln's speeches and writings and
liked especially the Gettysburg Address and the Second In-
augural. Indeed, Laurier shared with Lincoln a sense of mod-

eration and restraint and a belief in the virtues of friendly persuasion: first, as Lincoln wrote, you tried to reach a man's heart and then "you will find but little trouble in convincing his judgement of the justice of your cause, if indeed that cause really be a just one." You never presumed to dictate or command, for then your hearer would "retreat within himself, close all the avenues to his head and his heart". Laurier always followed this approach of Lincoln's instinctively, for he was a kind and reasonable man, like Lincoln.

Reading and the tranquil pleasure of life in Arthabaska could not satisfy Laurier indefinitely, however. While he and Zoë were still living at Dr Poisson's, Laurier was persuaded to run for election to the provincial legislature. He found himself in his element during the campaign, speaking out with assurance and conviction against the Catholic Program, education, even the Pope.

The Catholic Program had appeared in the spring of 1871 and was the work of a group of eager lay ultramontane followers of Bishops Bourget and LaFlèche. These enthusiasts were not content to destroy the *Rouges*; they looked forward to turning the Conservative party into a true Catholic party, which would be guided by the doctrines of the Church and consequently supported by all good Catholics. In the meantime they made one point extremely clear: in an election *any* Conservative candidate was to be supported in preference to a Liberal. This Program had a pretty wide appeal among the clergy, and the priests of Arthabaska were not immune. They joined the local *Bleu* paper in condemning the *Rouge* Laurier who believed in freedom of thought and action, who advocated doctrines condemned by the Church. "Let readers be on their guard!" the paper trumpeted. Despite this opposition, however, Laurier won with a good majority.

He began his political career as a member for Drummond-Arthabaska in November 1871 and his first speech was made three days after he took his seat. In moving the reply to the Speech from the Throne, a complacent affair that Laurier found no difficulty in attacking, he attracted attention with his easy eloquence. He deplored the economic condition of Quebec, the state of education, the emigration of young French Canadians to the United States, the backwardness of agriculture, the stagnation of industry. He urged French Canadians to become involved in commerce and industry, like English-speaking Canadians, and he thought that the old enmity between English- and French-speaking Canadians might well be changed into "generous emulation to excel each other in trade and industry, in the sciences and the arts of peace". He called upon the provincial government to encourage the development of industry through immigration: "What we need are the master miners of Wales and the north of England, the mechanics of Alsace, the Flemish weavers and the German artisans of all kinds." He wanted to waken French Canadians out of their lethargy. "We know only how to flatter our prejudices and our self-love," he said. "That is not true patriotism and it is not mine."

At the end of the second session in 1872, Le Pays wrote: "Mr Laurier has definitely carried off the sceptre of eloquence in the Legislative Assembly; I cannot, however, help reproaching him for not taking part often enough in the debates."

The Catholic Program was confusing provincial politics. The two ultramontane bishops who inspired it, Bourget and LaFlèche, were both tremendously vigorous men and their influence spread far and wide. Bishop Bourget advised: "Let each say this in his heart, 'I hear my curé, my curé hears the

bishop, the bishop hears the Pope, and the Pope hears Our
Lord Jesus Christ.' " What curés believed in the 1870s was
that good Catholics could not be Liberal. Some said plainly
that to vote Liberal was to commit a mortal sin. One priest
declared that "No Catholic could be a moderate Liberal:
moderate meant liar." Another pointed out what seemed to
him an obvious fact: Heaven was *Bleu*, and Hell was *Rouge.*

The Liberals responded to the attacks of the clergy in a
variety of ways. Extreme *Rouges* like Doutre fought hard
against the authority of the Church in the Guibord case.
Others, like Louis Jetté—a moderate and never an anti-clerical
Liberal—decided that soft answers would be more likely to
turn aside wrath. He and a number of friends attempted to
reorganize the *Rouges* as the *Parti National*; and in 1872 Jetté,
with ultramontane support, actually defeated Sir George
Etienne Cartier in the federal election in Montreal East. But
Jetté's success was not lasting; the *Parti National* soon declined.

The federal scene was becoming very interesting to Laurier. When the Pacific Scandal broke in 1873, and charges of
bribery and corruption against the Conservative government
reached right up to its head, Sir John A. Macdonald, it was
clear that its end was near. Macdonald resigned in November
and the Liberals under Alexander Mackenzie came to power.
A new election was not far off and there was now a vacant
seat in Drummond-Arthabaska. A deputation asked Laurier
to run for office, and even though he was ill, he eagerly rose
from his sickbed to campaign. The challenge and excitement,
far from injuring his health, seemed to help it. He not only
recovered but won the election, in January 1874, and entered
the House of Commons. He was to remain a member until his
death.

Laurier's first speech in the House, made on March 30, was in French, which might as well have been Greek to the majority of members. An English-speaking Liberal, James Young, observed him closely: "At first glance . . . he looked like an unsophisticated country boy. His long, chestnut-tinged hair naturally inclined to be thrown back on both sides and his clean-shaven face deepened the impression. Many supposed him much younger than he really was." He spoke "with all the self-possession of the practised orator—a charm of manner, a touch of dignity, an air of candour, a natural eloquence."

English-speaking members had a better chance of judging Laurier in April when he spoke in the House on the subject of Louis Riel, who had been elected to parliament in the Manitoba constituency of Provencher. Riel was the leader of the Métis—the French-speaking halfbreeds who lived in the Red River Settlement around present-day Winnipeg. When the people at Red River heard about the intended sale to the Canadian government of the Hudson's Bay Company terri-tories in the Northwest, they became worried about their future as part of Canada. Would the titles of their farms be secure? Would they have any control over the government to be established at the Red River Settlement? The Conservative government at Ottawa did nothing to allay their anxieties. To the Métis, who were accustomed to a semi-nomadic life based on the buffalo hunt, the future looked bleak. The great buffalo herds on whose existence they so largely depended were on the verge of extinction. In addition the Métis feared that once Red River was joined to Canada they would be confronted by hordes of English-speaking Protestant farmers from On-tario who would be contemptuous of them, just as the immigrants who had come from Ontario before 1869 were.

Their grievances were reported to Ottawa but nothing was done about them.

In December 1869 Riel and his Métis followers successfully resisted the authority of the Canadian government by occupying Fort Garry and preventing the Canadian-appointed Lieutenant-Governor elect, William McDougall, from entering Red River. Riel then organized a Provisional Government and managed to exact the Manitoba Act from the Conservative government in Ottawa. The Act was passed in the spring of 1870; it assured self-government to the newly created province of Manitoba, the Métis their lands, equal rights to the French and English languages, and separate schools. If this had been all, perhaps the whole affair would have appeared a triumphant assertion of popular rights, and no one would have rejoiced more in the outcome than the Liberals. Unfortunately during the course of the Red River Resistance a headstrong young Irishman from Ontario, an Orangeman named Thomas Scott, was tried by a Métis court martial and shot. Ontario, and particularly members of the Orange Order there, cried out in indignation. Edward Blake, for a short time the Liberal premier of Ontario in 1871, carried a resolution through the legislature offering $5000 for the arrest of Scott's "murderers". Quebec Liberals felt differently. They argued that a complete amnesty for all those involved in the Resistance at Red River was justified, since it had been caused by the negligence of the Conservative government. The Prime Minister, Sir John A. Macdonald, had been evasive on the question of the amnesty. He had sent money secretly to Riel so that he would leave the country and had later declared: "Where is Riel? God knows: I wish I could lay my hands on him!"

Riel was convinced that he had been promised an amnesty

and had declined to stay hidden. In March 1874, after being
elected to Provencher for the second time, he went to Ottawa, registered as a member of parliament, and took the
oath of allegiance before the clerk recognized him. He never
appeared in the House, however.

It was on the delicate question of expelling Riel that
Laurier made his first speech in English, on April 15, 1874.
He argued against the expulsion because the House of Commons had insufficient reason for demanding it, he said. The
matter of Riel's amnesty ought to be investigated before any
action was taken, for every British subject had the right to be
heard before being deprived of anything. Added Laurier, with
an artful appeal to English-speaking members, and yet with
perfect sincerity: "I am of French origin and my education
has been French, but I have of the Briton in me an ardent
love of fair play and of justice." He went on to say that the
execution of Thomas Scott, though a crime, was a political
act, made by a Provisional Government. "[Riel's] whole
crime and the crime of his friends was that they wanted to be
treated like British subjects and not to be bartered away like
common cattle. If that be an act of rebellion, where is the
one amongst us who, if he had happened to have been with
them, would not have been rebels as they were? Taken all in
all, I would regard the events at Red River in 1869-70 as
constituting a glorious page in our history, if unfortunately
they had not been stained with the blood of Thomas Scott.
But such is the state of human nature and of all that is
human: good and evil are constantly intermingled; the most
glorious cause is not free from impurity and the vilest may
have its noble side."

Laurier's speech was much admired, but it did not save
Riel from expulsion. And only in 1875 was a general amnesty

proclaimed by the Governor-General, Lord Dufferin—on his own, not the government's, authority. In Riel's case it was qualified by exile for five years.

Part of Riel's exile was spent secretly in Quebec—in asylums and sometimes with friends. During this time Laurier was invited to dinner at a neighbouring curé's to meet an "interesting guest". It was Riel. Laurier thought him vigorous and knowledgeable and fluent, but once the conversation turned to religion, Riel began to talk excitedly about his mission to reveal God's will, which a heavenly vision had made plain to him. Laurier then thought him mad and never changed his view.

Politics did not devour Laurier completely: he had his living to earn. In 1874 he formed a law partnership with Joseph Lavergne that was to last for more than twenty years. It prospered too, so much so that in a couple of years Wilfrid and Zoë were able to have a handsome red-brick house built for themselves. The tall windows on all sides kept the lovely countryside, in which they both delighted, constantly in view. There was only one big sorrow in their lives: no children were born to them, and they both loved children. But this regret was muted by a continual stream of visits from nephews and nieces, and from children in the neighbourhood. Both had much to absorb their energy and attention. Zoë Laurier managed the household and became an enthusiastic gardener. Laurier had his work and his reading.

The Lauriers were very much alive to the pleasures of nature that surrounded them at Arthabaska, but they also enjoyed the society of the lively little town. They became especially friendly with the large and independent-minded family of Pacauds. One of its members had turned Protestant rather than pay a certain portion of tithes that he felt his

The Laurier house in Arthabaska, Quebec

Church unjustly claimed; another left the Church after the dogma of infallibility was promulgated; most remained good, but never docile, Catholics. In young Ernest Pacaud, Laurier found a close friend and a warm supporter whose loyalty never failed. A niece of the Pacauds, Emilie Barthe, had lived abroad with her family for several years, mostly in Paris but also in London. One summer she came to Arthabaska on a visit and took the town by storm. In particular she captured the affections of Joseph Lavergne and stayed to marry him. Emilie Lavergne was not a beauty, but she had qualities that are more precious because they are more enduring—style and intelligence. It was her intelligence that captivated Laurier. He once compared her to Madame de Staël, "whose chief enjoyment is . . . to meet her friends, to have them about her, and then let the mind open its wings and fly about in the *arabesques* of improvised conversation".

In Ottawa Laurier advanced quickly, no doubt on his own merits but also because of the severe shortage of French-speaking Liberals. After Confederation the ranks of the *Rouges* had declined alarmingly. By 1875 the Liberal prime minister, Alexander Mackenzie, was looking desperately for a replacement for one of his *Rouge* cabinet members. His friend George Brown, the chief of Ontario Liberals before 1867, suggested "the young, vigorous, popular and eloquent man of the present moment—Laurier, I think is his name." But Mackenzie chose Joseph Cauchon because more of the Quebec Liberals seemed to prefer him. Cauchon was an ex-Conservative with a reputation for corruption—he was known to be interested in government contracts—but he had great appeal for the Liberals in 1875 because his relations with the Roman Catholic clergy were excellent. That merit had commanding importance in the 1870s, for the ultramon-

tane campaign against the Liberal party in Quebec was at its
height.

In the late 1870s the Liberals began to contest elections in
which clerical intimidation was especially striking; in 1876
they succeeded in getting Hector Langevin's election in
Charlevoix county annulled in the courts because members of
the clergy had broken the law forbidding "undue influence".
At this point Langevin was leader of the federal Conservatives, or *Bleus*, in Quebec; his brother was bishop of the
diocese that included Charlevoix. Getting Langevin's election
annulled was a triumph for the Liberals, but not of the sort
that would make the clergy more friendly. While Cauchon
was a Liberal cabinet minister he tried to solve the "holy
war" against the *Rouges* by having an apostolic delegate sent
out by Rome to bring peace to Quebec. In the spring of 1877
Bishop Conroy arrived in Canada to hear the opposing fac-
tions.

While Conroy was conducting his investigations, Laurier
decided to make his own contribution to ending the bad
relations between the *Rouges* and the Roman Catholic clerics. He accepted the invitation of the Young Men's Liberal
Association to speak at their meeting in Quebec City in June
1877 and chose as his subject "Political Liberalism". It
seemed a bold choice to Prime Minister Mackenzie and to the
Quebec *Rouges* in the cabinet. After reading an outline of his
intended speech, they asked him if he could postpone his
address until Conroy had ended his mission. Laurier replied
to the Prime Minister that he would be "as prudent as
possible. . . . It seems to me that if we cannot speak . . . plain
common-sense language, which we must have to speak some
day, the fate of our party is in a desperate condition."

On Sunday evening, June 22, before two thousand people

in the Salle de Musique, Laurier gave probably the most famous speech of his life. He began by defining the grave charges against the Liberal party in Quebec: that liberalism had been condemned by Pope Pius IX and that a Catholic could not be a Liberal. But, he declared, "Catholic liberalism is not political Liberalism", and he proceeded to make clear the folly of confusing the two. "We French Canadians are a conquered race. This truth is sad, but after all it is the truth. Yet, if we are a conquered race, we have also made a conquest: the conquest of liberty. We are a free people: we are a minority. But we have retained all our rights and all our privileges. Now, what is the cause to which we owe this liberty? It is the constitution which was won for us by our forefathers and which we enjoy today." Under that constitution citizens could choose their own government by voting in elections. But if the Catholics were not free to choose between the candidates of the two major parties, the Liberals and Conservatives, then the constitution would be a dead letter and there would be no freedom for French Canadians.

As for Liberalism, Laurier declared, it was no new idea but a principle almost inherent in human nature, as was Conservatism. "I am a Liberal. I am one of those who think that everywhere there are abuses to be reformed, new horizons to be opened up, and new forces to be developed." This did not mean that he believed in revolutions: "I hate revolutions and detest all attempts to win the triumph of opinions by violence." He preferred the way of the English Liberals who remedied abuses before they ever led to revolution, and he rejected the example of the liberals of Europe—"they are revolutionaries". Laurier conceded that the young Quebec *Rouges* of 1848 had been touched by enthusiasm for the European revolutionaries, but pointed out that the young men had grown older and more moderate, and the Liberal program had been revised until all that remained were "the principles of the English Liberal party". The clergy, having taken alarm in 1848, had stayed alarmed; and among Conservatives and Catholics there seemed to be a desire to organize a Catholic party. Laurier thought this dangerous, for it would encourage the organization of a Prostestant party, and then, "instead of the peace and harmony now prevailing between the different elements of the Canadian population, you throw open the door to war, a religious war, the most terrible of all wars".

On the other hand, Laurier thought the priest had every right to "speak and preach, as he thinks best". That right did not mean the priest could intimidate his parishioners, for "the constitution rests on the freely expressed wish of each elector". And surely that constitution ought to be upheld by all Catholics: "See if there is under the sun a country happier than ours; see if there is under the sun a country where the Catholic Church is freer or more privileged than it is here. Why, then, should you, by claiming rights incompatible with our state of society, expose this country to agitations of which it is impossible to foresee the consequences?"

It was a speech to hearten the *Rouges* and to please English-speaking Protestants, even if it did not convert the ultramontanes, bent on eradicating the *Rouges* and creating a Catholic party.

Interestingly enough, in October Bishop Conroy made the same distinction as Laurier between political and Catholic liberalism. In his report he reminded the clergy that it was forbidden to teach "from the pulpit or elsewhere that it is a sin to vote for any particular candidate or party; even more is it forbidden to announce that you will refuse the sacraments for this cause. You are never to give your personal opinion from the pulpit." Naturally the ultramontanes, who exalted the powers of the Pope, were rather cross at the judgement of the Pope's delegate. The struggle between ultramontanes and Liberals continued in the years ahead, but it became less open and vivid. Also, the ultramontanes were weakened by their failure to get Papal support.

In October 1877 Cauchon was appointed Lieutenant-Governor of Manitoba and Laurier entered the cabinet as Minister of Inland Revenue. Earlier he had expressed his reluctance to take this step. "The moment I accept office, I will go into it actively and earnestly, and from that moment my quietness and happiness will be gone. It will be a war with the clergy, a war of every day, of every moment . . . I will be denounced as Anti-Christ. You may laugh at that, but it is no laughing matter to us."

Laurier now had to face re-election in Drummond-Arthabaska, as every M.P. had to do on accepting a cabinet position. The Conservatives could have allowed this process to be a mere formality by simply not opposing his re-election. Instead they recognized Laurier's new importance by running a savage campaign against him. "Mr Laurier wants to make the priests marry," declared one ultramontane paper. Voters were assured that Laurier was going to Ottawa "to become a Protestant Minister". In the end bribery entered the contest. 3800 votes were cast in a constituency where there were only 3200 registered voters. Laurier was defeated by 29 votes. He was naturally very discouraged, though his feelings were not visible, according to the poet Louis Fréchette: "I was with him that evening. . . . We felt overwhelmed. Yet his good humour never varied by a hair's breadth from his habitual calm and his hand did not shake with the slightest quiver as he raised his glass in a toast to better days."

The Conservatives crowed in triumph over defeating the rising star of the Liberal party. Though the election had been corrupt, Laurier's lustre was dimmed a little. However, as he wrote to Mackenzie, "I am the last card of the party in this province. If I am sent down the party is well nigh gone down completely—at least our adversaries act under this assumption."

A place was found for Laurier in Quebec East and the eyes of the country were focussed on that constituency in a new election while the Liberals redoubled their energies to confront the still-determined Conservatives. Their efforts succeeded. One of the stories of this campaign tells of a *Rouge* who was warned by a *Bleu* that Liberalism meant people would march knee-deep in the blood of priests. "Oh well," said the *Rouge*, "we will put on high boots." A vociferous *Bleu* spokesman, Charles Thibeault, cried out at a meeting: "Laurier is disliked by the country, he is disliked by his home counties—and he is disliked by his wife!" An uproar ensued, and Thibeault's claim that he meant to say that Mme Laurier disliked Laurier's political career did nothing to repair the blunder. In the election on November 28, Laurier won—but only by a small majority, which the Quebec *Morning Chronicle* explained in the following way:

Many rumours, which we give with all reserve, are mentioned to account for the comparative meagreness of the majority of the Minister of Inland Revenue, as compared with the previous estimates of his friends. Among others, we quote the following:—

The ballot boxes of two polls were stolen in open violation of the law.

*A well-known St Roch's manufacturer who employs over
100 hands, most of whom were for Laurier, refused to give
them an opportunity to go to vote, dined them upon his own
premises, and stationed watchmen to prevent them from
escaping to record their votes for the man of their choice.*

*Over 300 good voters of the division were removed pre-
vious to the polling from the city by promises of work
elsewhere.*

*A noted shipbuilder checked his employees on Tuesday
night and discharged all those who were manly enough to
avow their contrary political opinions.*

*A number of the Deputy-Returning officers were notor-
iously enemies of the Ministerial candidate and their action,
frequently manifested in giving ignorant voters blank papers
in the usual envelopes instead of the legitimate ballots, was
more than once discovered. How many of these frauds escaped detection yet remains to be seen, but several of the
guilty parties are already marked for condign punishment.*

*Repeaters from Montreal and elsewhere were also num-
erous.*

"I have unfurled the Liberal Standard above the ancient
citadel of Quebec," Laurier proclaimed, "and there I will
keep it waving." In the years ahead, Quebec East would
always stand firm for him.

Early in December Laurier returned to Ottawa and a
triumphant reception. Though it rained, he was driven to
Mackenzie's house in an open carriage followed by hundreds
of other carriages and six hundred people who marched on
foot, while bands played and fireworks were shot off. The
Liberal leader waited for the procession on the verandah of
his house and when it arrived he welcomed Laurier by expres-
sing the conviction that now the Liberal banner could be

carried "over every province in the Dominion".

Laurier returned to Ottawa—a person of political consequence now, the most prominent Liberal in Quebec. He was
in time to enjoy the last session of a government that was
dying. The Prime Minister did not recognize that this was so,
however; he was pretty confident that his party would win
the election in 1878. His government had introduced many
important reforms. Above all it stood for "honesty, integrity,
and economy"—surely, Mackenzie thought, the highest qualities any administration could possess. Yet the country had
languished under a severe depression for five years: honesty
did not seem quite enough. The Conservative leader, Sir John
Macdonald, held out the lure of a National Policy of protective tariffs to encourage the growth of industry in Canada and
so develop the economy. The Liberals scoffed, for had not
Britain itself flourished under free trade, and was it not true
that high tariffs were paid by consumers and working men
for the profit of a few manufacturers? Still, the fact of the
depression was real. Moreover, Macdonald, whom the Pacific
Scandal of 1873 might have been expected to destroy, was
climbing back into public favour; he had more confidence
and spirit than ever. The phenomenon of a rejuvenated Macdonald reviving the Conservative party at one joyous election
picnic ground after another was something the Liberals had
not expected. They were beaten in 1878.

Mackenzie was shocked and withdrew in defeat. His party
grew restive. After an uncomfortable delegation told him of
dissatisfaction with his leadership, he resigned. Edward Blake
then became leader of the Liberal party, a position he held
from 1880 to 1887.

Blake was a curious politician. A remote intellectual, he
spoke of the leadership as a "crown of thorns". Since he was

short-sighted and often abstracted, he seemed to have a poor memory for faces. He was neurotic and frequently ill. His passion for accuracy led him to make long complicated speeches, leaving nothing for his followers to say. Twice he led his party to defeat, in 1882 and 1887. But he was incorruptibly honest and he had a brilliant mind. The Liberals, with only a few exceptions, adored him. Laurier observed of Blake that "without any of the lesser arts, he cast a spell over every man in parliament. We felt in the presence of genius, and would have been proud to serve to the end, had he not drawn himself aloof." Laurier was content to follow Blake's lead. He found this shy, difficult, brilliant man in rumpled tweeds deeply attractive, and the two became close personal friends.

There were many things in the early 1880s to discourage a Quebec Liberal. Federally the country seemed to be flourishing under Macdonald's National Policy, and the CPR was driving expensively and efficiently ahead. In Quebec the provincial Liberals floundered in defeat, as the federal Liberals had done. Not only were they opposed by a large and influential part of the clergy, but they lacked money. Sir George Etienne Cartier in his time had won a good deal of support for the *Bleus* from the business community, and with the *Bleus* it stayed.

Lack of money crippled the *Rouges* in many ways: they found it difficult to finance good newspapers, and without such support it was hard for them to get across to the electorate at all. Laurier, writing to Blake in 1882, listed twenty-five French papers in Quebec, of which only five were Liberal. Even this handful led "a very precarious existence, & no one is edited as it ought to be". Laurier knew all about the struggles of his friend Ernest Pacaud to keep publishing

his Liberal newspaper, *L'Electeur,* in Quebec City; in 1885 he
had to raise funds to save the paper from bankruptcy. Money
spoke louder than words at election time and in this respect
too the *Rouges* were at a terrible disadvantage. Laurier himself felt this when he was defeated in the Drummond-Arthabaska by-election of 1877: it took money to bring in the 600
strangers and the *Bleus* had it because business was on their
side. When the *Bleus* were in power—and they nearly always
were—they were careful to award government contracts on
advantageous terms to their business friends, who were then
happy to donate funds to the *Bleu* party. The *Rouges* found
it hard to make any headway against this "system". After the
provincial elections in 1881 Laurier wrote Blake despairingly:
"Corruption pervades every tissue of our society . . . The
English population in that respect is hardly better than our
own . . . You will readily admit that with a corrupt public
opinion, with money against us, with the clergy against us,
we must always be defeated. The greatest obstacle we have to
fight is the absence of honour, the lack of honesty in every
class of the population, especially the educated classes."

In the 1870s an ultramontane wing had emerged within
the Conservative party, organized by lay Catholics and devoted to maintaining the position of the Church against any
challengers. They came to be called *Castors.* Adolphe Chapleau, the brilliant and unscrupulous *Bleu* leader who became
premier of Quebec in 1879 and preferred railways to religion
in politics, detested them. He said the *Castors* were simply
"the ambitious mediocrities who cannot come to power by
the ordinary ways, all the disappointed ones, and a good
number of hypocrites who pretend to be religious and conservative in order better to ruin the great Conservative Party and
to destroy true religious spirit among the people. . . ." They

Edward Blake, 1878

had, he conceded, one thing in common with the true beaver: "They do their work with mud."

All things considered, Chapleau was tempted to drop the *Castors* and work out an alliance with the moderate *Rouges*, particularly with Honoré Mercier, another brilliant and ambitious politician. These two had something in common: both were stirring orators and could whip up crowds to feverish enthusiasm, and they were more interested in political success than politican reform. Unlike Laurier, they did not mind the corruption that "pervades every tissue of our society". Laurier, like other federal *Rouges*, was pretty glum about the possibility of such a coalition, and he managed to scotch it in a stirring attack on L.-A. Sénécal, Chapleau's intimate, who built expensive railways for the province of Quebec and who donated generously to the Conservative party. "The Den of the Forty Thieves", Laurier wrote, "is not in the heart of a forest . . . The robbers who seek refuge in it are not obscure bandits, hidden by day, prowling by night. On the contrary, they flaunt their shamelessness in the full light of day; they strut through the streets, they drink at the public bars, the smoke of their cigars is found on every hand. . . . This den of robbers is the administration of the Northern Railway, and the name of the chief of the band is Louis-Adélard Sénécal." Laurier went on to show just how expensively the railway had been built, how handsomely Sénécal had profited, and how he had shared his profits with the *Bleu* politicians in a number of ways—by issuing them free passes on the railway, for example, and by subsidizing their newspapers. The article was published anonymously in the new Liberal paper, *L'Electeur,* and Sénécal promptly brought a libel suit. Only at the trial did Laurier emerge as the author, and there he presented a brilliant indictment of

Sénécal's activities and won an acquittal.

Laurier's triumph in the court destroyed the prospective *Rouge-Bleu* alliance, but it did not destroy the *Bleus*. Chapleau went on to win the provincial elections in 1881, and in 1884 the federal *Bleus* refused to support a further subsidy to the CPR until Prime Minister Macdonald promised that the federal government would buy part of Sénécal's North Shore Railway from the provincial government. This piece of blackmail put the nearly bankrupt province of Quebec in funds again, and so restored the popularity of its *Bleu* government. It truly seemed, as Laurier wrote gloomily after the federal election in 1882, that "whatever cause there may be elsewhere for regret, there is also cause for hope, but we in Quebec have nothing to hope."

There was little a Liberal could do to change things. Laurier was content at this point in his career to lose himself in service to his leader and deskmate, Edward Blake, whom he admired enormously. He seemed unaware of disappointing people who looked to him for a brilliant career.

Young J.W. Dafoe, later to be the great Liberal editor of the Winnipeg *Free Press,* first observed Laurier in the session of 1884. "He was then in his forty-third year; but in the judgement of many his career was over. His interest in politics was, apparently, of the slightest. He was deskmate to Blake, who carried on a tremendous campaign that session against the government's CPR proposals. Laurier's political activities consisted chiefly of being an acting secretary of sorts to the Liberal leader. He kept his references in order; handed him Hansards and blue books in turn; summoned the pages to clear away the impedimenta and to keep the glass of water replenished—little services which it was clear he was glad to do for one who engaged his ardent affection and

admiration. There were memories in the House of Laurier's
eloquence, but memories only. During this session he was
almost silent. The tall, courtly figure was a familiar sight in
the chamber and in the library—particularly in the library,
where he could be found every day ensconced in some
congenial alcove; but the golden voice was silent. It was
known that his friends were concerned about his health."

Laurier was never a man to speak unless he had something
to say, or to act unless he had considered the consequences.
In politics he knew how to wait, and while waiting he showed
a great capacity for enjoying himself both in the library and
in society. His friendship with Emilie Lavergne became quite
intense, so that his law partner grew almost used to Laurier's
saying: "Joseph, if you will permit it I am going to talk with
your wife." And talk they did, for they were both bookish
and shared an enthusiasm for English culture. Emilie could
not forget her year in London. She took herself rather
seriously and was inclined to feel that she was Laurier's
mentor as well as his friend. Later she boasted that she had
taken "the little greenhorn of St Lin" and transformed him
into a man of the world. "He did not even know the correct
way to eat an orange at table. I made him understand that
this lack of etiquette would hamper him among the English
élite with whom he would be called to mingle at Ottawa."

The gossips of Arthabaska saw more than friendship between Emilie Lavergne and Wilfrid Laurier. They even affected to see a strong resemblance between Emilie Lavergne's
small son Armand and Laurier—but small towns are all alike
in their refusal to believe, as Laurier put it, "that there is
such a thing as chastity among women and honor among
men". Certainly Joseph Lavergne thought that no more than
friendship flourished between his wife and Laurier, and he

Emilie Lavergne, 1903

said so. As for Zoë, she gave no sign of hearing the gossip.

Laurier's tastes ranged far and wide. Once the Ontario Liberal, John Willison, was astonished to hear Laurier and Goldwin Smith "discuss treatises of French cookery with a familiarity as interesting as it was surprising". And Laurier's pleasure in parliamentary life was far from solemn. In 1884 he gave a speech in the rooms of the Montreal newspaper *La Patrie* and irreverently described the opening of parliament: "Nothing resembles a school more than Parliament. Nothing is more like the reopening of classes than the opening of Parliament. Despite the ten months of confinement to follow, the day of reopening of classes is always a gay one, and the same may be said of the day of the opening of the session. The pleasure of meeting each other again, the almost ceaseless handshaking, the exchange of more or less spicy jokes—all are to be found in Parliament just the same as in school on opening day." Then came "the Usher of the Black Rod ... to announce that the Governor-General desires the presence of the Commons in the Senate Chamber. Before opening his mouth, he advances nine steps, making three bows as he proceeds, and having delivered his message, he backs out repeating the same number of steps and of bows, wheels on his heels, and disappears, invariably accompanied by a formidable clapping of hands from all parts of the chamber." Added Laurier, with a certain rueful despair at the inscrutable ways of the English: "John Bull seems to take a perennial pleasure in seeing these bows made by a man paid to make them, and the same remark is repeated every year: 'Well, it is worth the money!' "

It was fortunate for Laurier that he took such pleasure in his life and his books, because there was not much amusement for a Quebec Liberal in the politics of 1884. There was no prospect of success, and to throw your heart into politics was surely to break it.

Then Riel turned up again, and everything changed.

Some Métis had now settled in the valley of the Saskatchewan. Distressed, as at Red River, by their failure to get secure titles to their lands, they once again appealed to Riel for help. He came to them in 1884 and drew up a petition that included the grievances of the Indians and white settlers as well as those of the Métis. Macdonald's procrastination and indifference and the Conservative government's policy of neglect were not to be changed overnight. In the West the pace was definitely faster, and by March 1885 Riel had organized a Provisional Government: in March also a group of Métis, led by Gabriel Dumont, attacked a force of North West Mounted Police at Duck Lake. This was the first battle of the Northwest Rebellion, which was all over by the end of May. It ended, as it inevitably had to end, in the defeat of the Métis and the Indians who had joined them by a large force of Canadians that had been rushed to the Northwest on the CPR. Riel made no effort to escape capture. His arrest was followed swiftly by his trial in Regina. He was found guilty of high treason, though the jury added a recommendation for mercy. After many delays he was hanged on November 16, 1885.

The consequences of Riel's execution were deep and pervasive. In Ontario there was little sympathy for Riel: he had led no less than two rebellions against the authority of the Dominion of Canada. The murder of Thomas Scott was not forgotten by the Orangemen of Ontario and the memory of the young Canadians who had died in 1885 putting down the rebellion was fresher still. Quebec had remained relatively calm about the rebellion itself, even after the capture of Riel, for it was widely assumed that Riel would be reprieved. The execution came as a deep shock and its effect endured throughout Laurier's career.

Alive, Riel had a deep concern for his people, the Métis, but very little for Canada. Dead, he divided Canada into Ontario and Quebec, English and French, as it had not been divided since 1867. He divided Liberals and Conservatives too. Macdonald managed to keep the French-Canadian cabinet ministers from resigning, but he could not keep the Quebec Conservatives from voting for the motion condemning the execution of Riel, a kinsman who had died for his defence of the French and Catholic minority in the Northwest. Edward Blake, who had long been trying to make the Liberal party less of an Ontario Protestant party, opposed the execution of Riel, but he could not carry all his party with him; many of the important Ontario Liberals supported the execution.

Laurier did not, and eloquently made clear why he did not. At a great meeting in Montreal, he declared ringingly: "Had I been born on the banks of the Saskatchewan . . . I would myself have shouldered a musket to fight against the neglect of governments and the shameless greed of speculators." In other speeches he explained carefully that there were no rebellions without cause, and that the Rebellion of 1885 in the Northwest was the plain result of the Conservative government's neglect: this provided Riel with followers as nothing else could have. He added: "But this I say, and I say it coming from a province where less than 50 years ago every man of the race to which I belong was a rebel, and where today every man of that race is a true and loyal subject, as true and loyal as any that breathes—I say give these men justice, give them freedom, give them their rights, treat them as for the last 40 years you have treated the people of Lower Canada, and by-and-by, throughout those Territories, you will have contentment, peace and harmony where today discord, hatred and war are ruining the land." Vengeance, not justice, caused the execution of Riel, whom Laurier and Blake and all the Quebec Liberals believed insane: "The death of Scott is the cause of the death of Riel today." But what Canada really needed was a policy of reconciliation, not vengeance: "We are a new nation, we are attempting to unite the different conflicting elements which we have into a nation. Shall we ever succeed if the bond of union is to be revenge?"

Laurier spoke his mind on the Riel question not only to sympathetic French audiences and within the sanctuary of parliament; he addressed hostile audiences in Toronto and elsewhere, like the one here described.

During the local elections of 1886, there was a great meeting held of the English-speaking electors of Megantic. Fanaticism had done its work; the Orangemen, by means of the Riel question, had aroused the prejudices of the Protestant element against us. One of our friends was concluding his speech, when an Orangeman of the place shouted out in a rage: "None of you have spoken of Riel and none of you will dare to do so!" Yells arose, vociferations broke out, in all directions. Laurier simply replied: "I will." And, worming himself into their sympathies by an appeal to British loyalty and by reminding them of the spirit of tolerance and justice which would animate all the citizens of a mixed country, he related to them the details of the dark tragedy in the North West.

We have been told that that hostile crowd bowed their heads not wholly convinced, but tamed, subjugated by the courage of the man and the eloquence of the orator.

The Riel question brought Laurier strongly to the fore-front again, but it did surprisingly little for the federal Liberal party since it was as divided on the execution as were the Conservatives. What it did was allow Mercier, leader of the moderate *Rouges*, to win a plurality in the next provincial election in Quebec as leader of a nationalist movement, a re-created *Parti National,* which would unite all French Canadians in defence of their national rights. He was supported by some members of the *Castor* or ultramontane wing of the provincial Conservative party and formed a coalition government with them in 1887. The *Castors,* who were as ardent French-Canadian patriots as they were Roman Catholics, were outraged by the execution of Riel. In the years ahead Mercier was able to bind them to his *Parti National* by stressing the nationalist, not the liberal, part of the *Rouge* tradition.

When Laurier demanded justice and freedom for the Métis, he spoke more as a liberal intellectual than a French-Canadian patriot. He seemed cool compared to Mercier, the passionate and eloquent French-Canadian nationalist. In the federal elections of 1887, the Liberals lost again, though in Quebec they improved their standing.

3

Leader of the Liberals

Right after the election of 1887 Blake informed his fellow Liberals that he meant to resign the leadership of the party. He had nearly destroyed his health in the mighty campaign and was depressed by the election results. The Liberals were appalled by his announcement. They urged him not to think of resigning, for there was no other possible leader. "If you give up the leadership," Laurier wrote to him, "there is no one to take your place; chaos and confusion must prevail, and the disruption of the party must finally ensue."

It is easy to read history backwards and to suppose that Laurier's abilities must have shone brightly in 1887, but in fact they did not. Blake eclipsed all other Liberal stars. His intellect and energy and high principles made him the pride of Ontario Liberals, but his appeal went beyond Ontario. Quebec Liberals found him a very sympathetic leader. They liked him for opposing the incorporation of the anti-Catholic Orange Order; they approved his support of a motion favouring Home Rule for Ireland; and they were deeply impressed by his opposition to the hanging of Louis Riel. Consequently they were very upset at the idea of his resignation, for there was a possibility that he might be succeeded by Sir Richard Cartwright or David Mills, Ontario Liberals who had favoured the execution of Riel. One Quebec Liberal, François Langelier, urged Blake not to resign because "nobody else enjoys to the same degree the esteem of the most influential portion of our clergy and people. . . . Another difficulty would be to find another leader. Laurier would scarcely do on account of his want of physical strength." L.H. Davies of Prince Edward Island said much the same thing. "Poor, dear Laurier, a more charming fellow never lived. I would stand by him and fight for him . . . but it would be the veriest piece of political Quixotism." Most of the Liberals admired Laurier's eloquence, but they thought him frail and indolent, not nearly tough or energetic enough to be leader of the Liberal party.

Blake was persuaded to remain as leader for the parliamentary session of 1887. But on June 1 he resigned firmly—and forever, as it turned out. Cartwright thought of himself as the next leader, but to the parliamentary Liberals who asked Blake's advice in choosing his successor, Blake declared: "There is only one possible choice—Laurier."

Laurier did not feel this, either then or later. He argued that he had neither the wealth nor health to sustain him in so difficult a role. He felt it would be a mistake to have a French-Canadian leader in a country with an English-Canadian majority, particularly in view of the continuing hostility between English and French, between Ontario and Quebec, reawakened after the execution of Louis Riel. When he learned that Blake had named him as his choice for leader, he visited Blake in his home that very evening. Blake was ill, reclining on a sofa, his wife at his side. Laurier enumerated all the reasons why he thought he would be a poor choice, but Blake simply repeated what he had said before: Laurier was the only man. "Yes, Mr Laurier," said his wife, "you are the only man for it."

At a secret party caucus on June 7 Cartwright nominated

Laurier as leader and Mills was the seconder.* But Laurier did not formally accept the leadership until June 23.

Public response, as expected, was mixed. It ranged from the comments of *La Minerve*, which regretted "the replacing of a giant by a pygmy", and the Victoria *Weekly Colonist*, which called the appointment an "egregious error", through the cautious approval of the Toronto *Globe*—it wrote "all may safely reckon that trial will not find Mr Laurier wanting in any respect"—to the enthusiasm of *La Patrie*, which said that one great Canadian had replaced another.

Laurier did not settle into the job of leader with any satisfaction. In fact he said he wanted to resign after the first session of parliament. He found no pleasure in the position; he did not have an income that could support it—he was neglecting his practice and suffering financially. He urged Blake to return.

His first real ordeal as leader came in the summer of 1888 when, accompanied by Zoë, he made a speaking tour of some Ontario towns in the central and western parts of the province. He was not at his best; he could not relate to his audiences there. For this reason he seldom made a favourable impression on them. One occasion when he did occurred when an Anglican clergyman in the audience shouted out that you could not learn the true way from a Roman Catholic. "You could—in politics," Laurier replied, and proceeded to silence the clergyman so effectively that he was later congratulated by John Willison of the Toronto *Globe*: "You should have that preacher for all your meetings," he said, and Laurier laughed. But the tour as a whole convinced him more

* "They [Cartwright and Mills] were slow, however, to admit that caucus had acted wisely, and for years their speeches contained no eulogy of the leader." John Willison, *Reminiscences*.

Wilfrid Laurier, about 1882

than ever that he was the wrong man to be leader. Willison was one of Laurier's warmest Ontario supporters and yet he wrote: "I cannot think . . . that his reputation was enhanced . . . and I am confident that he did nothing to dispel the common notion among Liberals that he was too gentle and too gentlemanly for the hard, rough, uncompromising, aggressive warfare in which a political leader must engage if he is to establish his own position, control a party in parliament, and inspire respect and devotion in the constituencies."

— The coolness towards Laurier in Ontario was not due mainly to his personality. When he rose to speak it was the French Canadian from Quebec that his audiences thought about, not the national leader of their party. Things had been happening in that province to arouse mistrust in every Ontario Liberal (and Conservative), and Laurier could not be dissociated from these events in the often prejudiced minds of his listeners.

Mercier became premier of Quebec early in 1887. He did not precisely deny Laurier's claim that "we are French Canadians, but our country is not confined to the territory overshadowed by the citadel of Quebec; our country is Canada", but he did tend to act as if *his* country were Quebec. His flamboyant leadership united not only the *Parti National* but almost all of Quebec. It also alarmed Ontario.

Mercier embarked on an energetic program of settling French Canadians on new lands within Quebec, appointing the popular curé, Antoine Labelle, as Deputy Minister of Colonization. This program did very well in Quebec but it was scarcely applauded in Protestant Ontario, easily alarmed by priests and really appalled at the idea of their being in the government, even the Quebec government. But what caused a much sharper reaction in Ontario was Mercier's policy in

connection with the Jesuits' Estates. This was an old problem; it went back to the conquest of New France when the
Jesuits' possessions had passed to the British Crown. In fact
the British government did not take over the Estates until
after the death of the last surviving Jesuit, well after the
Order had been suppressed by Pope Clement XIV in 1773. In
1831 the Jesuits' Estates were given to Lower Canada to be
used for education, both Catholic and Protestant; and at
Confederation their control passed to the province of Quebec. A good part of the Roman Catholic clergy was never
satisfied with this arrangement and felt strongly that the
Jesuits' Estates ought to be given to the Church in Quebec,
for the benefit of the dioceses in which they existed. Meanwhile the Pope had lifted the ban on the Order, and in the
1840s the Jesuits returned to Canada. Not unnaturally they
were interested in recovering their long-lost properties. Mercier, who had been educated by the Jesuits at St Mary's
College in Montreal, was kindly disposed to them. In 1887 he
introduced a bill to settle the dispute between the various
claimants of the Estates. By it, the province of Quebec was to
grant $60,000 to the Protestant schools as compensation for
their share in the revenues of the Estates, and $400,000 was
to be divided by the Pope between the Roman Catholic
Church in Quebec and the Jesuit Order.

Mercier's solution seemed to benefit all parties—even the
province of Quebec, for the Jesuits' Estates were valued at
two million dollars, and the government settled the claims of
the Jesuit Order and the Roman Catholic clergy for less than
a quarter of this amount. Yet Mercier's Jesuits' Estates bill
was opposed by large and influential portions of Ontario.
Perhaps the reaction would not have been so strong if some
order other than the Jesuits had been involved, for English

Protestants hated and feared the Jesuit Order beyond all others: it was to them "an alien association, hostile to free institutions". The appeal to the Pope to settle the division of the Estates seemed like a particularly unattractive form of foreign intervention to ardent Ontario Protestants like the Conservative D'Alton McCarthy and the Liberal John Charlton.

Mercier, however—unlike Macdonald and Laurier in Ottawa—was not trying to win golden opinions in Ontario but rather in Quebec; and in Quebec he succeeded.

In Ontario, Mercier's Jesuits' Estates Act led straight to the formation of the Equal Rights Association* by McCarthy and other aroused Protestants, and to a great agitation for the disallowance of the Act by the federal parliament. However, only thirteen M.P.s—the "Noble Thirteen" or the "Devil's Dozen", as they were variously called—voted for disallowance, so that Macdonald was perhaps justified in writing almost soothingly to the Governor-General: "One of those insane crazes . . . has taken possession of the ultra Protestants which can only be compared with the Popish Plot or the papal aggression agitation. . . . The drum ecclesiastic is beating in all parts of Ontario. Dislike of the French has much to do with the excitement, which I think will soon die out, but I shouldn't like a general election just now." The Equal Rights Association, determined to make Canada a British country, extended its campaign to western Canada. D'Alton McCarthy attacked the place of the French language and of separate schools in Manitoba and the North West Territories, with heavy consequences for the future.

Laurier had felt for some time that he should speak in

---

* The name was anomolous. It referred not to equality of rights but to the supremacy of English and of state, as opposed to separate, schools.

Toronto, unsympathetic to him though it was, and a meeting
was arranged for him in September 1889. He braved a crowd
of McCarthyite hecklers to argue against disallowance because it interfered with the province's right to settle the
question, and he even defended the settlement itself. The
audience was hostile but he won a hearing and his courage
was admired. Willison commented on the impression he
made: "He is very, very firm; a calm, strong, steadfast man
who will not be turned from his purpose. . . . This man would
be a giant in some great national crisis."

From the time he became leader, Laurier realized that
some "bold policy" was needed to make a success of the
Liberal party and of himself as leader. Turning away from the
racial quarrels that were bringing the young Dominion close
to disintegration, he directed his attention to the economy.
Laurier was no businessman and was really not very interested in economic questions, but the agitation sweeping Ontario for commercial union with the United States caught his
politican's eye. "We must try to make a new departure," he
wrote to Blake in January 1888. "There is really a deep
discontent everywhere. In this province I never saw business
so dull as it is now. All classes are in more straitened circumstances than they have ever been within my experience.
There is a universal desire for change. Commercial union
would afford relief & commercial union must be popular. It
is the general desire that we should make it a party issue."

Reciprocity always had been attractive to Canadians, for it
recalled the golden age in the 1850s when there had been free
trade in natural products between Canada and the United
States and Canada had flourished. Both Liberals and Conservatives thought of recriprocity with respect and tried in vain
to get the agreement renewed after 1866: the Americans

became firmly protectionist and built ever-higher tariff walls. Partly in imitation of the American example and partly in retaliation, the Conservatives turned to the National Policy of protective tariffs to build up a national economy in Canada, but in the late 1880s this policy had failed to duplicate the American success story. The West was not filling up with immigrants, even though the CPR was available to transport them; factories in central Canada were not growing fast enough to prevent a good deal of emigration to the United States; and everywhere the prices of farm products were low. The United States looked attractive; its markets for Canadian products were nearly irresistible. Hence there arose an enthusiasm, in Ontario and the Maritimes particularly, for ending all tariff barriers between the two countries. There were even those—like the brilliant Oxford don, Goldwin Smith, a very displaced citizen of Toronto—who wanted to go beyond commercial union to political union with the United States.

In 1888 the Liberals adopted a modified version of commercial union and called it Unrestricted Reciprocity. They urged that all customs barriers between the United States and Canada should be removed, but that each country should retain its own tariffs against other countries. Sir Richard Cartwright, the Liberals' chief financial critic and long the terror of Canadian manufacturers because he hated the tariffs that protected them from foreign competition, was naturally an ardent supporter of Unrestricted Reciprocity; and Goldwin Smith observed in his sharp, unsympathetic way that Cartwright was the real leader in Ontario, a position he retained through the combined weakness and good temper of Laurier. But Laurier did not dislike the policy, nor fear that it would lead to annexation.

In the election of 1891 the Liberals campaigned vigorously

in favour of Unrestricted Reciprocity, which carried them straight to defeat. The Conservatives succeeded in convincing people that Unrestricted Reciprocity would lead to annexation with the United States: it was a disloyal policy, even treasonable. Sir John Macdonald grandly declared: "A British subject I was born, a British subject I will die. With my utmost strength, with my last breath, will I oppose the 'veiled treason' which attempts by sordid means and mercenary proffers to lure our people from their allegiance." The Conservatives' charges of disloyalty were strengthened when they produced a copy of a pamphlet by one of the Liberal *Globe*'s editorial writers, Edward Farrer. Farrer had written the pamphlet at the request of an American friend and for private circulation; in it he explained how Americans could induce Canada to enter the American union. The exposure of Farrer's pamphlet destroyed the large victory the Liberals had so confidently expected in 1891. All the same, the Conservatives did little more than break even in Ontario and Quebec, winning their majority from the Maritimes and the West— "the shreds and patches" of the Dominion, as Sir Richard Cartwright observed with characteristic tactlessness.

Right after the election of 1891, Edward Blake published a letter to his constituents in West Durham that ruined any chance the Liberals had of winning the by-elections that followed the general election after the courts controverted a number of the returns. The letter was long and complicated, but it revealed that Blake thought Unrestricted Reciprocity would lead straight to political union with the United States, just as the Conservatives charged. This condemnation from Blake—Laurier called it "a stab in the back"—destroyed the morale of the Ontario Liberals for a time. It also proved to be the end of Blake's connection with the Liberal party, and this may well have strengthened Laurier's position as leader. Blake had been a distracting presence in the House of Commons after 1887, for many Liberals had continued to look to him as the real leader of the party. After the West Durham letter, his influence lessened. In June 1892 Blake accepted the invitation of the Irish Nationalists to help them in their struggle to win Home Rule and he took a seat in the British House of Commons.

The friendship of Blake and Laurier survived the West Durham letter, though after its publication there was no communication between the two for a few months. In the summer of 1891 Laurier found an occasion to consult Blake and to express his hope that "divergence in political views will not affect personal friendship". To Emilie Lavergne who, like the Blakes, was spending the summer at Murray Bay, he explained that "[Blake's] letter on the political situation is a slap in the face of the party and of me particularly. I cannot be angry with him: I know him too well and love him too well." A few days later he warned her not to reproach Blake with the West Durham letter, for "if he had the slightest conception how deeply he can wound, his good heart will only suffer more." Blake himself felt keenly his ostracism by all the Ontario Liberals except Mills and was eager to restore his friendship with Laurier: "Not being the brute devoid of natural affections which some politicians have made me out, but a man perhaps more than ordinarily dependent for my happiness on my friendships, I am not ashamed to say that I have suffered heavily." Laurier understood Blake's scrupulous temperament and admired his high sense of honour—the very qualities that caused him to speak his mind in the West Durham letter.

Shortly after the election of 1891, Sir John A. Macdonald

died. Langevin announced the death of his old friend and ally
to the House of Commons, but found he could not speak at
length: "My heart is full of tears," he said. It was left to
Laurier to find words for those strong emotions: "The place
of Sir John Macdonald in this country is so large and so
absorbing that it is almost impossible to conceive that the
political life of this country—the fate of this country—can
continue without him. His loss overwhelms this Parliament,
as if indeed one of the institutions of the land had given
way."*

— After Macdonald's death, the Conservative party proceeded gracelessly to collapse. One agent of destruction was
the Quebec journalist, Israel Tarte, who had the reputation of
being a brilliant if unscrupulous party organizer. He had been
an ultramontane *Bleu* and a devoted supporter of Sir Hector
Langevin, Minister of Public Works, but in 1891 he was
elected as an Independent. That same year, in his newspaper
Le Canadien, Tarte destroyed his former chief by well-docu-
mented revelations of corruption in the Public Works Department. Much of the story centred on the activities of the
McGreevy brothers, Thomas and Robert. Thomas was wonderfully successful in seeing that government contracts were
awarded to the firm to which his younger brother Robert
belonged. Robert, in turn, saw that very generous donations
were made to the Conservative party in Quebec, whose treas-
urer was Thomas. Thomas McGreevy also happened to be a

---

* We have a record of what Macdonald thought of Laurier in this anecdote from Sir
Joseph Pope, given in *The Day of Sir John Macdonald:* "About a month before
Sir John Macdonald died Mr Laurier came to his office in the House of Commons
to discuss some question of adjournment. When he had gone, the Chief said to
me: 'Nice chap, that. If I were twenty years younger he'd be my colleague.'
'Perhaps he may be yet, sir,' I remarked. 'Too old,' said he, 'too old,' and passed
into the inner room."

close friend of Langevin's. How far Langevin was involved in these activities was never made fully clear, but his connection was close enough to ruin his chances of succeeding Macdonald as Prime Minister.

Despite the political advantages to the Liberals, Laurier was not able to take much pleasure in the McGreevy-Langevin scandals. "To accuse, to recriminate, to hurt, to wound is not congenial to my nature," he wrote to Emilie Lavergne at the time, "and all this must be performed within the next few weeks. It is a stern duty: it has to be done, and though the men against whom it has to be done are nothing to me, it is a task which I detest." Even if Laurier had delighted in the affair, the pleasure would have been short-lived because Mercier's government in Quebec was also involved in scandal —exactly the same sort of scandal, involving contractors and kickbacks, that the Liberals had been relentless in criticizing the Conservatives for.

The federal Liberals were not directly involved in the provincial scandal, but all the same Mercier was a *Rouge*. Laurier felt crushed. It seemed that there was little to choose between Liberal and Conservative morality. "Tell me", he wrote to Honoré Beaugrand, editor of the Montreal Liberal paper *La Patrie*, "whether there is not some fatality pursuing our party."

After Macdonald's death Senator John Abbott became Prime Minister—because, as he said with engaging frankness, "I am not particularly obnoxious to anybody." A year later Abbott resigned and was succeeded by Sir John Thompson, a thoroughly able man whose chief defect in the eyes of Ontario was that he was a Roman Catholic convert—considered a worse fault by ardent Protestants than being born a Roman Catholic. Laurier admired Thompson, but found little in the politics of the early 1890s to please him. He detested Ottawa; in 1892 he found it "duller this year than I have ever seen it. On the few occasions that I have been out, I have not met a soul worth remembering." He shrank into his rooms at the Russell Hotel, reading steadily to keep his mind off the uninspiring scenes around him and writing long, affectionate letters to Emilie Lavergne. "Invariably while I am here, these beautiful days of spring make me long . . . to get away, and find myself once more—and all of a sudden if possible—in those hills where my heart is. This day I experience that feeling as keenly as, if not more keenly than, ever."

His warm affection for Emilie Lavergne embraced her children as well. He delighted in Gabrielle, fretting whenever he heard she was sick, and he took a serious interest in Armand's scholarly progress. Laurier thought Armand "a real infant Macaulay", though the boy insisted on seeing himself as a French-Canadian *patriote* with a strong disinclination to learn English. Laurier was amused, but urged his mother to "tell him that above everything else, he must apply himself to learn English, that it is absolutely essential for such an intense French Canadian as he is; that it is the absolute condition which will enable him, some day, to defend the rights and privileges of his race. That ought to fetch him."

Perhaps Ottawa brightened up a bit for Laurier after the arrival in 1893 of a new Governor-General, the gentle Lord Aberdeen, and his impulsive, warm-hearted, and energetic wife. They were both Gladstonian Liberals, with an earnest desire to do good work in the world. Lady Aberdeen found Ottawa very hard to take at first, and she chased away her blues "by putting up a picture of Mr G[ladstone] in every room". This activity may well have had a less than cheering effect on Canadian Conservatives; all the same both Aberdeens took the Prime Minister, Sir John Thompson, and his family to their hearts. They were much shocked by Thompson's sudden death at Windsor Castle in December 1894 and were unfailingly kind and helpful to his family both at the time and in the years that followed. They were not attracted to his successor, Sir Mackenzie Bowell, after whose appointment evil days came for the Conservative party—"days which I never recall without a blush", wrote Sir Joseph Pope, secretary and biographer of Sir John Macdonald, loyal Conservative, and also a friend of Laurier's—"days of weak and incompetent administration by a cabinet presided over by a man whose sudden and unlooked-for elevation had visibly turned his head, a ministry without unity or cohesion of any kind, a prey to internal dissensions until they became a spectacle to the world, to angels and to men."

Under the circumstances, the Aberdeens could scarcely fail to be struck by Laurier. They first met him shortly after their arrival in Canada, at which time Lady Aberdeen noted in her *Journal* that he was "a brilliant speaker, a man much respected by both sides". The day following the introduction they met him again—at Dawson's the booksellers, characteristically. Just after Thompson's death, Lady Aberdeen wrote that "now the Liberals are exceedingly likely to be successful, taking all things into consideration, & Laurier's attractive personality & eloquence contrasted to the want of any strong man or even any outstanding figure amongst the crowd of common-places in the Cabinet." Laurier's merits did not diminish in the months ahead. And Zoë Laurier's qualities began to be recognized too. Lady Aberdeen took the Lauriers in hand. "Am trying to doctor M. Laurier for his indigestion as he will not see a doctor," she noted in her *Journal* on January 16, 1896. A month later, at an enormously elaborate

fancy-dress ball given by the Aberdeens, Mme Laurier led the
bourrée, representing "the days of Maisonneuve & the founders of Montreal". Lady Aberdeen noted approvingly that at a
tea she gave for one of the Thompson girls, Lady Thompson
"particularly appreciated Mme Laurier coming & being very
warm to her".

— Meanwhile Conservative disintegration proceeded apace.
Early in January 1896 a large part of the cabinet rebelled
against Prime Minister Bowell's leadership and was enticed
into unity, partly by the fear that Lord Aberdeen would call
on Laurier and the Liberals if they did not unite, and partly
by Bowell's promise that Sir Charles Tupper would take over
the leadership of the party at the end of the session. Tupper,
who had been serving as High Commissioner in London, was
an old warhorse of astounding energies. He returned to the
House of Commons in February 1896, but not in time to
rally his disunited forces and lead them to victory in the next
election.

— The Conservative party came to grief over the Manitoba
schools question. Ironically it was D'Alton McCarthy, himself
a Conservative, who made a controversy out of this. The
Manitoba Act of 1870 had placed French and English on
equal footing as the official languages of the province, and
had provided for the establishment of Protestant and Roman
Catholic school systems. Until 1889 Manitobans went on
living peacefully enough under the provisions of the Act,
even though Manitoba was settled largely by Ontario Protestants and the French Roman Catholic minority remained
small. Then, during the summer of 1889, D'Alton McCarthy
made a rousing anti-Catholic speech at Portage la Prairie, to
which at least the Liberal government of Manitoba responded. Early in 1890 legislation was passed abolishing French as

an official language and ending the dual system of education. The Assembly of the Northwest pursued the same ends by asking the federal government to repeal the rights of the French language in the Northwest Territories.

The federal government was confronted first by the question of the place of French in the Territories. In a stirring speech D'Alton McCarthy made it abundantly clear that the abolition of French-language rights, established in the North West Territories in 1875, was just the beginning of an "Equal Rights" campaign. "This is a British country," he declared, "and the sooner we take up our French Canadians and make them British, the less trouble we will leave for posterity." The French-Canadian M.P.s were appalled by McCarthy. Not very many English-speaking M.P.s were attracted; most of them felt that the people who actually lived in the Northwest ought to be free to decide the language question for themselves, and a majority in the Commons voted for an amendment to this effect. What this meant was that the French language would swiftly be abolished in the Northwest, for the majority there was English-speaking. Laurier spoke strongly against McCarthy's object, but all the same he supported the amendment to allow Northwesterners to arrange matters for themselves. It was, he urged in a letter to a Quebec friend, "a necessity for the people of Quebec province to maintain inviolate the principle of local autonomy".

The Manitoba schools legislation took longer to reach the federal parliament than the question of French-language rights in the Northwest, but when it finally arrived its effect was far more devastating. The Conservative government had encouraged the distressed French Roman Catholic minority to appeal to the courts to decide whether the Manitoba Liberal government's school acts were legal; and for some

years the courts wrestled with the question of whether the
Manitoba government had the right to abolish a school system that seemingly conformed to the provisions of the Manitoba Act. Then the courts turned to consider whether the
parliament of Canada had the right to pass legislation to
redress the grievances of the French-Catholic minority. Finally the last court decided the last question: the Judicial
Committee of the Privy Council of Great Britain said yes, the
federal government could act to restore the educational privileges—separate schools—that the minority had lost by the
Manitoba School Acts of 1890.

It was not a joyful occasion for the Conservative government. Its Ontario members were becoming infected by the
passions of the Equal Rights Association; its Quebec members hardened their determination to see justice done to the
French Catholics in Manitoba. In 1895 the Conservative
government sent a remedial Order-in-Council to the Liberal
government of Manitoba, directing it to restore the Roman
Catholic schools, to allow these schools to share in the
provincial grants, and to exempt Roman Catholics from supporting other schools. The Manitoba government replied neg-
atively at very great length and invited the federal government to investigate; but commissioners sent by the federal
government were unable to work out an agreement. The
Manitoba government, under Premier Greenway, seemed prepared to discuss the matter forever; freshly re-elected to
office, it did seem to have all the time in the world. For the
federal Conservatives, however, time was running out, and
the party was torn by dissension. Prime Minister Bowell
proposed a Remedial Bill to help the Catholic minority in
Manitoba; but not all the determination of his successor, Sir
Charles Tupper, could get the bill passed before the session

ended and the federal election campaign began. In the campaign of 1896 half the Conservative candidates in Ontario were pledged to vote against any remedial bill in the next parliament, so that maybe voters were justified in taking with a grain of salt Tupper's promise to come to the aid of the French-Catholic minority of Manitoba.

The Liberals needed to do very little about the Manitoba Schools question except sit back and enjoy the spectacle of the harassed Conservatives trying endlessly and failing continually to find a satisfactory solution. Being in opposition, they were under far less pressure than the Conservatives. Initially they had agreed with the Conservatives that the courts ought first to decide whether the Manitoba legislation was legal. Laurier really favoured the restoration of the separate-school system, but he was well aware that he lived in an imperfect world and that the best was often unavailable. He was a realist, and a cool one at that; for years he did little to make clear his views on the question. Rather he emphasized the need for investigation, and after the remedial order was sent to the Liberal government of Manitoba in 1895, he attacked the coercive style of the Conservative government. "The government are very windy", he observed in a speech in Morrisburg, Ontario. "They have blown and raged and threatened and the more they have raged and blown, the more that man Greenway has stuck to his coat. If it were in my power, I would try the sunny way. I would approach this man Greenway with the sunny way of patriotism, asking him to be just and to be fair, asking him to be generous to the minority, in order that we may have peace among all the creeds and races which it has pleased God to bring upon this corner of our common country." When the Remedial Bill was introduced in the session of 1896, Laurier made a motion to

adjourn the discussion for six months; he opposed the dicta-
torial nature of the bill and urged that it would never accomplish half so much as "sunny ways", that investigation and
conciliation were the only sure means of arriving at a solution
everyone would accept.

— In recommending this approach, Laurier moved onto the
sure Liberal ground of provincial rights, for ever since Confederation the Liberals had attacked the centralizing policies
of Sir John Macdonald, who had a tendency to regard provincial governments as minor institutions, deeply subordinate to
the federal government. Liberal champions of provincial
rights had risen to power in province after province, first and
most enduringly in Ontario, where the Liberal premier, Oliver
Mowat, had for years waged war in the courts—and with
success—to make clear that the provinces were supreme within their own spheres, one of which was education. Manitoba
had a particularly strong feeling for provincial rights; for
years its government fought against the federal government's
policy of protecting the CPR by disallowing construction of
lines south to the American border. The provincial government wanted to grant railway charters as it pleased.

— The French Roman Catholic bishops were not, however,
very interested in provincial rights. They wanted to have their
lost schools in Manitoba restored—the question seemed to
them religious, not political—and the Remedial Bill seemed
an obvious solution. They were inclined to press for its
adoption, and in a collective pastoral issued in the spring of
1896 they urged all Catholics to vote for candidates who
pledged support for the Remedial Bill. Earlier Father La-
combe, a much-respected and beloved missionary in the West,
had written to Laurier: "It is in the name of our bishop, of
the hierarchy and the Catholics of Canada, that we ask the

party of which you are the very worthy chief to assist us in settling this famous question, and to do so by voting with the government on the Remedial Bill. . . . If, which may God not grant, you do not believe it to be your duty to accede to our just demands . . . I inform you, with regret, that the episcopacy, like one man, united with the clergy, will rise to support those who may have fallen in defending us."

To this Laurier replied in parliament: "No. So long as I have a seat in this House, so long as I occupy the position I do now, whenever it shall become my duty to take a stand upon any question whatever, that stand I will take not upon grounds of Roman Catholicism, not upon the grounds of Protestantism, but upon the grounds which can appeal to the conscience of all men, irrespective of their particular faith, upon grounds which can be occupied by all men who love justice, freedom and toleration." No doubt this statement was designed to reassure Protestant Ontario, nervous about voting for a French Roman Catholic in the approaching elections. But there is no doubt that Laurier meant what he said. His words provoked a severe reply from the ultramontane Bishop LaFlèche: "There is the most categorical affirmation of the Liberalism condemned by the Church which has ever been made, to my knowledge, in a Legislative Assembly of our country. The man who speaks thus is a rationalist Liberal. He formulates a doctrine entirely opposed to the Catholic doctrine; that is to say, that a Catholic is not bound to be a Catholic in his public life. It is a fundamental error, which can lead to the most deplorable consequences."

Not all the Roman Catholics in Quebec were ultramontanes, nor were they persuaded that the Remedial Bill, even if it were passed by the federal parliament, would achieve its object: the re-establishment of the separate schools in Manitoba. As for the hierarchy, in Quebec it may have stood "like one man" in support of the Remedial Bill; outside Quebec it did not.

— The Liberals won the election of 1896 partly because they fought a badly divided Conservative party, which was so like Humpty Dumpty that not even Sir Charles Tupper could put it together again. In Quebec the Conservatives were without any effective leaders. Langevin had retired after the McGreevy scandals. His rival, Adolphe Chapleau, the lieutenant-governor of Quebec, could not be coaxed by Tupper into organizing a great Conservative campaign against Laurier, because by 1896 he did not object to Laurier's winning. The two had something in common. They both disliked the ultramontane *Bleus,* and neither was ever attracted, as Mercier was, by the idea of Quebec as a separate state. All through the 1880s Chapleau had tried and failed to unite Quebec under his leadership of the Conservative party, as Cartier had before him, with the object of co-operating with sympathetic English-speaking Canadians on matters of common interest. Laurier, as Liberal leader, had much the same object in mind. In 1894, he had written: "I believe that I shall continue the work of Mr LaFontaine and Sir George Etienne Cartier and the result will be all to the advantage of French Canada." The sick and discouraged Chapleau seemed to believe this too, and his close associate, Israel Tarte, set to work to organize the Liberal victory in 1896, saying: "Leave Quebec to Laurier and me." Where this erratic *Bleu* led, others followed. The Liberals won 49 of the 65 seats in Quebec. Laurier won the support of the great majority of French Canadians, who were captivated by the idea of a French-Canadian prime minister. Most of them were accustomed to supporting the *Bleu* party, but in 1896 there was no *Bleu* party—there was only a group of rigid ultramontanes, ineffectual politicians every one. So most of the *Bleu* vote went to Laurier, who was after all a moderate Liberal and no red republican.

Quebec was the great cornerstone of the Liberals' victory in 1896, although elsewhere they did well enough, except for Manitoba, where the Conservatives won 4 of the 6 seats in the province they were supposed to be coercing. The Liberals came out of the elections with a comfortable majority of 30. Laurier perhaps found it hard to believe that the long night of opposition was over. He had often doubted his ability to lead his party to victory—as late as 1895 he had written, "an English leader would be much stronger than I can ever be", and just two months before the elections he had offered the leadership to Mowat.

Prime Minister Tupper perhaps found his defeat difficult to believe too, though he gave no sign that he did. "I shall never forget", wrote Sir Joseph Pope, "the jaunty air with which that intrepid old man came down to his office the morning after the battle, nor the brave and resolute manner in which he faced the reverse which he must have realized at his age meant the death-knell of his ambitions and hopes." He had a first-class quarrel with Lord Aberdeen, who refused to make all the last-minute appointments that Tupper pressed on him. Finally, on July 9, Sir Charles Tupper presented his resignation to the Governor-General. (On this occasion his manner was cross, not jaunty.) Then Lord Aberdeen called on Laurier to form a government, and he became the first French-Canadian prime minister of Canada.

4

The Prime Minister

Laurier was prompt in forming his first cabinet; by July 13, 1896 all but three of the seventeen ministers had been sworn in. During eighteen years of opposition the Liberal party had accumulated many people whose claim for office was high and whose desire for it was keen. In cutting through the various claims of ability and accomplishment, of region, religion and race, to form a strong cabinet in so few days, Laurier revealed from the outset a crisp and confident authority as prime minister. Power changed Laurier. He lost none of his charm or kindliness of disposition in the process of taking hold—he remained on friendly terms with those he passed over in choosing his cabinet—but he made it clear from the beginning that his judgement was unaffected by sentiment.

In Quebec Laurier's right-hand man, Israel Tarte, became chief of the Quebec members in the cabinet as Minister of Public Works. Tarte had done more than anyone else to organize the Liberal victory in Quebec in 1896. He symbolized the union between the Chapleau *Bleus,* the real heirs of Cartier, and the Laurier *Rouges.* As for the old *Rouges*—loyal warriors through the dark years when the Liberals were in opposition—they were mostly excluded or given minor posts.

C.A. Geoffrion became Minister without Portfolio—"the mat before the door", as he described his position sourly. François Langelier did not get in the cabinet at all, even though he had fought Liberal battles for thirty years. Perhaps he brought old quarrels with the Church too vividly to mind. Langelier and his friends disliked being left out, and hated particularly to see their old enemy Tarte as the head of the Quebec group within the cabinet. Laurier was unmoved by their protests. He was tough-minded, not sentimental, in his cabinet making: the Chapleau *Bleus* had to be kept in the Liberal party if the Liberals meant to continue winning Quebec elections, and every other consideration was secondary. In time, Laurier managed to soothe the outraged tempers and feelings of the *Rouges* by a skilful application of judicial appointments; but in 1896 shouts of joy were mingled with cries of rage.

Among Ontario Liberals also there were bitter disappointments. Sir Richard Cartwright was one of the chief sufferers. He had been Minister of Finance from 1874 to 1878, and through the long years of opposition he had been the chief financial critic of the Liberal party; he had every reason to expect to become Minister of Finance again. Instead Laurier offered him the much-less-important ministry of Trade and Commerce. Maybe this was Cartwright's reward for years of frightening Canadian manufacturers with the promise of low tariffs, or for promoting Unrestricted Reciprocity with such fatal results for the Liberals in 1891; he may also have called to mind too vividly the lean years of opposition. In any event he and other old Ontario Liberals got very small tastes of the sweets of office. One Ontario Liberal who did make it into the cabinet was William Mulock, who became an extremely competent Postmaster General. His nickname was "Farmer

Bill", and he really did have a farm, but in fact he was a lawyer with Toronto business interests.

Laurier was careful to include in his cabinet representatives of each of the main races, religions, and regions. Some of its most talented members were former provincial premiers. Oliver Mowat had been premier of Ontario for twenty-four years: any ship of state in which he was included seemed utterly seaworthy and impeccably steered. He became Minister of Justice and lent instant respectability to the government. But Mowat was an old man. More important for the future was the ex-premier of Nova Scotia, W.S. Fielding, who became a very able Minister of Finance, the leading English-speaking member in Laurier's cabinet, and his closest associate. Another Maritime premier, A.G. Blair of New Brunswick, became Minister of Railways and Canals.

Altogether Laurier's first cabinet sparkled with ability. It also reflected his determination to re-establish the credit of the government of Canada that years of scandal and quarrelling under the Conservatives had done much to destroy.

➤ The first great question that Laurier and his new cabinet had to settle involved the Manitoba schools. The Liberals had promised French-speaking Canadians that the educational grievances of the Roman Catholic minority in Manitoba would be redressed, and English-speaking Canadians that Manitoba's right to control its own system of education would not be interfered with. They had agreed with Laurier that "sunny ways" would really be more helpful to the French Roman Catholic minority than any number of blusterous orders from Ottawa, and that a compromise could be worked out that would have the support of the whole Manitoba community. Laurier was very concerned to show the truth of the Liberals' case. He brought to bear on th

HON. SIR LOUIS H. DAVIES, M.P.,
Minister of Marine and Fisheries.

HON. W. S. FIELDING, M.P.,
Minister of Finance.

HON. A. G. BLAIR, M.P.,
Minister of Railways and Canals.

HON. CLIFFORD SIFTON, M.P.,
Minister of the Interior.

RT. HON. SIR WILFRID LAURIER, G.C.M.G., M.P.,
Prime Minister and President of the Council.

HON. J. I. TARTE, M.P.,
Minister of Public Works.

HON. DAVID MILLS, Senate,
Minister of Justice.

HON. WM. MULLOCK, M.P.,
Postmaster General.

HON. SIR RICHARD CARTWRIGHT,
G.C.M.G., M.P.,
Minister of Trade and Commerce.

Lamefield Photos.

Wilfrid Laurier and leading members of his cabinet, 1899

question some of his best talents—Mowat from Ontario, who for years had managed to treat with liberality the French Canadians within Ontario, and Israel Tarte, whose energy and enthusiasm no one ever did deny. In Manitoba, Clifford Sifton, who had brusquely rejected all changes proposed earlier by federal Conservatives, found it possible to arrange a compromise with his fellow Liberals from Ottawa; after the schools settlement was worked out, he was rewarded with a cabinet appointment as Minister of the Interior in the Liberal government.

The Laurier-Greenway settlement was a compromise. The French Roman Catholics of Manitoba did not get their schools back, but they did get some rights within the public-school system. Religious teaching was allowed in the last half-hour of the school day; Roman Catholic teachers could be chosen when there were a certain number of Roman Catholic children; teaching could be partly in French (or some other language) when that was the language of the children being taught. To most Canadians—even to D'Alton McCarthy and to most Roman Catholic bishops in Canada—it seemed a pretty good compromise, but not to Bishop Langevin of Manitoba nor to the French Catholic bishops of Quebec; they turned on the Liberals with fury, condemning politicians and newspapers alike.

It was the 1870s all over again. Among the victims was *La Patrie,* published by the sons of Israel Tarte. In parliament, Tarte explained just what the Church's condemnation meant: "In the diocese of Chicoutimi there is not one Roman Catholic who goes to confession without being asked if he is a subscriber to my sons' paper. . . . If the answer is in the affirmative the man is told that he has to send back the paper or that he will be refused the sacraments of the Church."

Laurier defended the Manitoba school question with spirit, and was as opposed to clerical intimidation as he had been in the 1870s. "Nothing", he said, "will deter me from continuing to the end in my task of preserving at all cost our civil liberty." The "active and violent intervention of the clergy in the domain of political questions" Laurier decided to treat as a religious, not a political problem. Together with forty-four other Roman Catholic Liberal members of the Commons and Senate he petitioned to Rome to bring to an end the clerical warfare which, "if allowed to continue, might be extremely dangerous to the constitutional liberties of this country, as well as to the interests of the Church itself." Pope Leo XIII appointed Monsignor Merry del Val as apostolic delegate and he spent some months in Canada investigating the dispute.

Monsignor Merry del Val made no public statements, but even before he returned to Rome, clerical agitation began to subside. The papal encyclical, *Affari Vos*, released in December 1897, recognized the justice of the protests, but not the wisdom of clerical intimidation. The Laurier-Greenway settlement, it declared, was "defective, imperfect, insufficient", yet "partial satisfaction" ought not to be refused. Complete justice must be worked for, not with bitterness but with "moderation, gentleness, and brotherly love". The storm died down in Quebec, yet hostility only appeared to disappear: there remained many clerics who had never loved the Liberals and never would. All the same, most Canadians approved of the Liberals' settlement of the Manitoba schools question. French Canadians were pleased at the very real concessions Laurier was able to win for the Catholic minority in Manitoba; and English-speaking Canadians were delighted that Manitoba's right to control education within the province remained intact.

Meanwhile the Liberals had been dealing with other matters close to the hearts of a great many Canadians—trade and finance.

Fielding's first budget as Minister of Finance was presented in April 1897 and it excited a good deal of attention. The Liberals, particularly in English-speaking Canada, had long given the impression of being a distinctly low-tariff party. Cartwright, for example, called the tariff "the absolute foe of all freedom" and condemned as endlessly corrupting the high tariffs introduced by Macdonald's government to protect Canadian industry from foreign competition. Even though he was a good deal more insistent than most Liberals and the party had moderated its tariff policy at the convention of 1893, free trade remained an ideal to many, and lower tariffs both practical and desirable. Even though Fielding was not Cartwright, sweeping changes were expected in his budget. In fact the changes were few and minor: no one could call them sweeping. Some duties were abolished—on binder twine, for example; others were reduced—on coal oil; still others were actually increased—on pig iron. Fielding carefully explained (just as Blake had years before) that revenues from tariffs were the chief source of government income, and that they had to be retained to meet the costs of running the government. His realism was supplemented by an imaginative measure that combined the Liberals' enthusiasm for lower tariffs with the general Canadian feeling of loyalty to Great Britain. The measure was complicated, but what it amounted to was this: an "imperial preference"—lower tariffs—was offered on goods imported from Great Britain. Free traders and imperialists in both Canada and Great Britain were delighted, for to both groups it seemed a step in the right direction, even if they did not agree on the direction. Free traders thought lower tariffs would eventually lead to no tariffs, and imperialists thought the Imperial Preference would lead towards the unification of the Empire. It seemed a kind of recognition of Queen Victoria's Diamond Jubilee. Rudyard Kipling wrote a poem about this free gift from Canada, oldest of the self-governing colonies, part of which went:

> *A Nation spoke to a Nation,*
> *A Queen sent word to a throne:*
> *"Daughter am I in my mother's house,*
> *But mistress in my own.*
> *The gates are mine to open,*
> *As the gates are mine to close,*
> *And I set my house in order,"*
> *Said our Lady of the Snows.*

The *New York Times* correspondent wrote from London: "The spirit of preference for the Mother Country appeals to the imagination here. This change will make Mr Laurier, when he comes here in June, far and away the most conspicuous and popular of all the visiting Premiers of the Empire." This indeed turned out to be the case when Laurier attended the Diamond Jubilee celebration in London: the Imperial Preference prepared the way for a triumphant reception. He and Zoë sailed for England in June—it was their first ocean crossing—and when Laurier arrived he was treated as the central colonial visitor.

The great Jubilee celebration, attended by loyal subjects from the four corners of the world, both reflected and caused an outburst of imperial sentiment. Laurier shared in this warmly, since he believed that the British Empire stood for liberty and justice in the world. He had long been the devoted admirer of English politics, an attentive reader of

English historians like Macaulay. Years before he had written to an English-speaking Liberal: "As you follow in Macaulay's pages that constant struggle between liberty and despotism and the slow and steady progress and at last complete triumph of liberty, the student of French history is struck with amazement. This is the reason why I admire you so much, you Anglo-Saxons."

The British were struck by Laurier's elegant appearance and graceful manners and particularly by the romantic background of the French Canadian whose ancestors had been defeated by the British in 1759 and who had risen to be Prime Minister of Canada. That he admired British institutions also endeared him to them strongly. Indeed, they lionized him.

Laurier and Zoë were swept along on a hectic round of receptions, dinners, and balls. "I am not sure whether the British Empire needs a new constitution," he wrote to a friend back home, "but I am certain that every Jubilee guest will need one." He entered into the celebration with enthusiasm. The high point for him was his visit to W.E. Gladstone, whom he thought the greatest statesman of the nineteenth century because of "his intense humanity, his paramount sense of right, his abhorrence of injustice, wrong, and oppression wherever to be found or in whatever shape they might show themselves." Laurier received honorary degrees from Oxford and Cambridge, and on June 21, after a state dinner at Buckingham Palace, he was knighted by the Queen.

The knighthood was accepted reluctantly. Laurier had wanted to decline the honour—one that Blake and Mackenzie had refused out of a spirit of equalitarianism—but he was finally persuaded to accept it. His friend Joseph Pope recalled the resulting "fuss" that was made in Canada:

"A democrat to the hilt," he had always described himself.
Years afterwards he spoke to me about this, in explanation of
his course. He said that when he got over to England, he
found all arrangements made for his acceptance of the hon-
our, that his acquiescence was taken for granted by the
Queen, and that to refuse at the last hour would have been a
boorish act and one deeply resented by Her Majesty.

Laurier once said that the knighthood was "a serious
political error, and I have never ceased to regret it".

On June 22 there unfolded in the streets of London the
kind of pageant that only the English can produce. In the
early morning the rulers, princes, and other notables from
Britain's colonies, each with a panoply of colourfully dressed
troops, gathered for the long parade. There were Cypriots
and Dyaks and Zouaves and Haussas and Sikhs and Chinese
and Maltese and Singhalese and Malays, as well as British
colonists from Canada, New Zealand, Queensland, New
South Wales, the Cape of Good Hope, South Australia—the
list went on and on. A son-in-law of Queen Victoria's "could
not help remembering that no sovereign since the fall of
Rome could muster subjects from so many and such distant
colonies all over the world." Laurier rode with Zoë in a
carriage at the head of the Colonial Procession, escorted by
the Governor-General's Guard, the Toronto Grenadiers, and
the Royal Canadian Highlanders. At its rear marched a unit
of the scarlet-jacketed North West Mounted Police. Then
came the Royal Procession. All were heading for St Paul's
Cathedral, before which a short outdoor service of thanks-
giving was held (for the Empire, for the Queen's long reign).
It seemed to Laurier that "a quiver of emotion ran through
all that crowd, and each of us felt a deep-seated conviction
that, unlike the Roman Empire, which, having been raised by

violence, succumbed to violence, the British Empire, based
on eternal laws of liberty and justice, will live forever". On
the return journey Laurier's carriage immediately followed
that of the old Queen.

Right after the Jubilee celebrations the British Colonial
Secretary, Joseph Chamberlain, met the prime ministers of all
the self-governing colonies at the Colonial Conference and set
before them his plans for achieving imperial unity. Chamberlain was not a sentimental man, but he thought the imperial
enthusiasm of the Jubilee year ought to be turned to account. He thought the British Empire should be organized, its
energies united, and the self-governing colonies given a share
in running the imperial government. In this way British
power would be increased to meet the new challenges hurry-
ing towards it from Germany and the United States and
Russia. Chamberlain felt sure that the British would prevail—
"that proud, persistent, self-asserting and resolute stock . . . is
infallibly destined to be the predominating force in the future
history and civilization of the world"—but all the same, work
was needed to make a glorious future certain. Chamberlain
proposed to work towards imperial unity by establishing "a
great Council of the Empire"; he requested too that colonies
contribute to the imperial navy. Laurier rejected both these
proposals politely but firmly. There were a number of nation-
alistically inclined Canadian imperialists who were distressed
that Canadians had no control over foreign policy or defence
and argued that a share in making imperial foreign policy was
much better than nothing at all; but Laurier felt that any
share Canadians might have would be extremely slight, and
that, far from giving Canadians greater control over their own
destiny, an imperial council would simply bind Canada more
closely to British destinies. Like most nineteenth-century

British Liberals, Laurier believed that the natural destiny of British colonies was independence; but he was in no hurry to push towards this inevitable future. On the other hand, he didn't mean to push away from it, so he took the lead in rejecting Chamberlain's plans to unite the Empire. This division between Laurier and Chamberlain did not become public at the time; the Colonial Conference ended amicably to all appearances, since its members declared their common resolve to meet periodically in the future. For Canadians the chief result seemed to be another triumph for Laurier: the British government decided to take advantage of the Imperial Preference offered by Canada and took the essential first step by renouncing trade treaties with Germany and Belgium.

Before Sir Wilfrid Laurier and his wife returned to Canada they visited France—a very cool and distant France at first, for the French were quarrelling with England and inclined to be hostile to the French Canadian who sang praises of the British so insistently and so often. But after a couple of speeches and a few interviews with members of the French government, Laurier transformed the atmosphere. His method was characteristic. He did not deny or qualify any of his earlier speeches, but explained exactly why the French Canadians were loyal to the British connection, and then went on to express the deep and continuing admiration that French Canadians felt for France. "We are faithful to the great nation which gave us life, we are faithful to the great nation which has given us liberty." Laurier carried conviction because he spoke with conviction. The French presented him with the ribbon of the Legion of Honour.

All Canada was delighted by the reception Laurier had won for himself and for his country in Great Britain and France. Welcoming bonfires burned all along the banks of the

The Lauriers entertain Lord and Lady Aberdeen at Arthabaska, 1897

St Lawrence between Quebec and Montreal to honour the Lauriers on their return from Europe. Gifts arrived in such quantities that Zoë Laurier protested she would need a new house to hold them. In fact, there was to be a new house. The Liberal party, grateful for Laurier's election victory in 1896, was providing one, and at the same time Mulock had seen to it that a fund to "protect you from want the rest of your days" was established. Nothing succeeds like success. The Jubilee proved that too. Boards of Trade in Montreal and Toronto arranged banquets in Laurier's honour. French and English Canadians sang his praises with equal fervour.

This happy feeling of unity did not last, however, because there was a real division between French- and English-speaking Canadians on the subject of Empire. At the turn of the century, English-speaking Canadians were stirred by racial pride at the thought of Anglo-Saxon achievements, and were intensely proud of the imperial connection. Many shared Chamberlain's desire to unite the Empire so that the British could continue to bring "the blessings of civilization, freedom and peace" to the four corners of the world. Laurier recognized the strength of English Canadians' devotion to the Empire; but he also realized that French Canadians would never happily endure being plunged into Chamberlain's Empire. The French Canadians too had a sense of racial pride and as clear a feeling of mission as English-speaking Canadians. "This religious and civilizing mission is . . . the special vocation of the French race in America," said Monsignor Pâquet. Racist themselves, French Canadians were repelled by the racism that the new wave of Anglo-Saxon imperialism embodied.

The division between French- and English-speaking Canadians on the subject of the Empire became clear in 1899 during the Boer War. Why Canada should become involved in a war in South Africa was not at all clear at the outset, for Canadian interests were not immediately involved and Canadians had never been accustomed to contribute to all of Britain's wars. In 1885 Macdonald had refused to send troops to help the British in the Sudan because Canadian interests were not involved: "Why should we waste money and men in this wretched business?" he had said. Laurier was inclined to follow Macdonald's example. He came to feel that justice was on the British side, that the Boer government was wrong in its treatment of its British subjects; still, he did not think that Canadians ought to contribute to the British cause. Lord Minto, the new Governor-General in Canada and a rational imperialist, agreed. He wrote to his brother: "From the point of view of a Canadian statesman, I don't see why they should commit their country to the expenditure of lives and money for a quarrel not threatening imperial safety."

Chamberlain thought quite differently. He wanted to establish British control in South Africa and to show the unity and strength of the Empire: the Boer War was to be a great imperial occasion, the Jubilee repeated in blood and iron. And so he pressed the Canadian government for a contribution. Such pressure Laurier was ready and willing to resist; what he found irresistible was the enthusiasm of English-speaking Canadians. Domestic, not imperial, pressure finally caused the Laurier government to abandon its policy of non-intervention. In the fall of 1899, the Liberal cabinet issued an Order-in-Council that authorized the sending of a contingent of volunteers to South Africa, to be equipped and transported at the expense of the Canadian government. This seemed a reasonable compromise between the ardent desire of English Canadians to go and of French Canadians to stay home. It was not, however, to be "construed as a precedent for future action", the Order-in-Council concluded in a rather strained effort to soothe French Canadians who had no desire whatever to be involved in any British imperial wars that did not clearly affect Canadian interests. To a great many Canadians the Liberal government's policy during the Boer War was another successful realization of Laurier's own policy of conciliation between the races.

There were critics, however, and the most important was Henri Bourassa. A young man of thirty-one in 1899, he was the grandson of Louis-Joseph Papineau and, like him, a *Patriote*. He was first elected to the House of Commons in 1896. His formidable intelligence and his clear, critical mind attracted Laurier, who singled him out as a possible future leader. He was chosen as an aide to Tarte during the Manitoba Schools negotiations and was named Secretary of a Joint High Commission that met in 1898 to settle problems in American-Canadian relations.

In 1899 Bourassa resigned from the Liberal party because of his opposition to Canada's participation in the Boer war. He opposed the Liberal government for liberal, not French nationalist, reasons, though he was in fact an ardent nationalist. Unlike Laurier, but like many Liberals in England, Bourassa thought the British cause in South Africa wrong. In his view Chamberlain and the imperialists were trying to assert British power, not justice, in South Africa. And he saw no reason at all why Canada should be involved in helping British militarists crush the small Dutch population whose only sin seemed to be a stubborn desire to live independent of British rule. Canada was in the war not because of the decision of its parliament but because the Liberal government had yielded to British pressures; and this opened up a dangerous future. "If we send 2,000 men and spend $2,000,000 to fight . . . a population of 250,000 souls, how many men shall we send, and how many millions shall we expend to fight a first-class power or a coalition of powers?" Bourassa argued that the cabinet's Order-in-Council authorizing the sending of troops to South Africa constituted a dangerous precedent; and that the new policy of involvement ought not to be adopted behind the closed doors of a cabinet meeting but discussed and accepted by parliament and people.

Shortly before Bourassa resigned, he had questioned Laurier closely about his decision to send troops to the Boer War without consulting parliament. The Prime Minister replied at length, finally concluding wearily: "My dear Henri . . . the circumstances are difficult." Bourassa leapt on this with his customary vigour, saying: "To govern is to have the courage, at a given moment, to risk power to save a principle." Laurier might well have resented being called to task by so young a man, but he gave no sign of it. He merely said: "Ah, my dear young friend, you have not a practical mind."

In parliament Laurier made a reasoned defence of his policy. He claimed that Canadians were taking part in the Boer War not because of British pressure on the government but because a great many Canadians desired this involvement; and that in the future, as in the past, Canada would decide her own policy. "Whilst I cannot admit that Canada should take part in all the wars of Great Britain, neither am I prepared to say that she should not take part in any war at all. . . . I claim for Canada this, that in future she shall be at liberty to act or not act, to interfere or not interfere, to do just as she pleases." Privately he wrote to Bourassa: "Tell me, what attitude should the French Canadians take in the Confederation? They must isolate themselves as a separate body or march at the head of the Confederation. It is necessary that we choose between English imperialism and American imperialism. I see no other alternative. If there is one I wish you would indicate it to me." Really what Bourassa wanted was for the nineteenth century to continue a little longer. He liked the old British Empire, powerful and unassailed, which protected Canada and allowed it the luxury of security without the expense of paying for it. He detested the new British imperialism and he feared American imperialism: he did not want to choose between them.

Laurier was distressed by Bourassa's resignation, for he hated to lose so talented a young man: "It is a personal chagrin, more than just chagrin, to be separated from you. I had hoped for other things." The political division between the two deepened, yet neither wanted a complete break. Towards the end of 1900, Laurier was writing to Bourassa: "I hope you will not come to town without giving me the pleasure of chatting with you for a moment. . . . We can agree to disagree." To his young sister-in-law, inclined to be critical of Bourassa, he said: "Don't speak ill of him . . . he is young, and he has much talent."

Bourassa's anxieties about British imperialism were probably shared by a great many French Canadians, but there was no great organized opposition in Quebec to Laurier's policy of sending volunteers to South Africa. In the general elections of 1900 the Liberals won 58 of the 65 seats in that province. Laurier remained the idol of his race, but after 1900 Bourassa, now an Independent, watched him closely and critically to see just how well and truly he served the interests of his fellow French Canadians. The real opposition to Laurier came from Ontario imperialists who were both critical and influential. It seemed to them that Laurier had

THE DIFFERENCE IN THE MEN.

SIR CHARLES—He is one of those absurd fellows who has what they call an "Ideal"—really believes something, you know, in dead earnest ; preposterously ridiculous I call it.

FOSTER—Yes, goes in for "statesmanship" as if Canada was really a nation—it makes me laugh!

This election cartoon appeared in the *Globe*, Toronto, 22 October 1900, and shows Laurier, the champion of Union, Peace, Friendship and Fraternity, being derided for his high ideals by two members of the Opposition: Sir Charles Tupper, the Conservative leader, and Sir George Foster—both of whom were defeated in the November election.

been too reluctant to help the British in South Africa, and that the Canadian contribution had been both late and small. In 1900 the Liberals won only 34 of the 92 seats in Ontario, the province that had once been the very heart and soul of the party.

The loss of Bourassa in Quebec and of fourteen seats in imperialist Ontario could not obscure the strong Liberal victory in 1900, not only in Quebec but in the Maritimes and western Canada. After 1900 imperialist passions subsided.

In 1902 Laurier again went to London, to attend the coronation of Edward VII and—a far more severe ordeal— another Colonial Conference presided over by Joseph Chamberlain. The pageant, though impressive, was clouded by the Boer War. The British had found it unexpectedly difficult to win, and so the glory of Empire was a little dimmed. Even Chamberlain struck a sombre note. "The weary Titan staggers under the too vast orb of his fate," he said, as he invited the self-governing colonies to share with Britain the costs of imperial defence. He promised at the same time a share in running the Empire: the colonies would be represented on a "real Council of the Empire".

Laurier resisted all Chamberlain's plans to unite the Empire. He refused a peerage. Even his speeches were more guarded: his oratory did not flow like champagne. Maybe his lack of sparkle had something to do with his health. He was desperately sick, and as soon as the formal engagements were got through, Laurier hurried to seek the advice of doctors on the continent. They feared cancer.

Laurier's sickness affected only his mood, not his mind. Even before Laurier left Canada, he had declared his determination to keep his country out of "the vortex of militarism which is the curse and the blight of Europe". He had no

desire whatever to become entangled in Chamberlain's empire. To British imperialists he was a bitter disappointment:
one of them declared "the damn dancin' master . . . bitched
the whole show."

Canadians didn't seem to mind at all. In Laurier's absence
Israel Tarte had been providing rare entertainment. He was
still the unrivalled party manager in Quebec and chief repre-
sentative of the alliance with the *Bleus* that Laurier thought
so essential to Liberal success; he had every reason to consider himself indispensable in the cabinet. But he was not the
kind of person who could lie still in the sun for long. He liked
to be up and doing. His colleagues had some experience of
this, for as Minister of Public Works Tarte had frequently
encroached on the concerns of other departments. He had
always been a protectionist, and in the summer of 1902 he
campaigned all across Ontario for higher tariffs. He delight-
edly received enthusiastic praise and backing from business-
men. The Liberal paper *Le Soleil* observed his progress with
less enthusiasm: "Sweating, puffing, panting, he did not
merely run, he flew, he whirled, from North Bay to Essex—
for Ontario was the key to success." "Laurier is better
loved," Tarte said, "but I have the great interests behind
me." It seemed to many that Tarte was determined to succeed the ailing Laurier, but this view was not shared by his
fellow cabinet members. They thought that Tarte was on the
rampage again, determined to drag the whole government
after him, and were deeply indignant at his behaviour.

Laurier understood Tarte but shared his colleagues' reaction. He returned on October 18 and Tarte was fired the
next day. In a crisp letter Laurier pointed out that cabinet
ministers were not crusading newspaper editors; they could
not give way to private enthusiasms without consulting fel-

low cabinet members, or considering the Liberal policy.

For the time being imperial questions did not excite much attention. Tarte and most Canadians were agreed on one point: their major interest was the development of their own country. Its possibilities seemed endless. The dramatic change from the depression that clouded the Conservatives' last years in office began shortly after the Liberals came to power in 1896. Laurier, of course, did not create the economic boom that Canada began to enjoy: he had no magic touch. The end of the supply of free land in the United States helped bring immigrants to western Canada. New kinds of wheat were developed that flourished in the short growing seasons of the Northwest, and wheat growing became not only possible but profitable because industrial Europe needed more and more imported wheat. Great Britain in particular imported Canadian wheat and invested in Canadian development, especially railway building.

All the same the economic boom seemed to be a Liberal one, and this was because Laurier's cabinet members took over the direction of Canadian economic development with such energy and enthusiasm. No one was more active than Clifford Sifton of Manitoba, Minister of the Interior and the only westerner in the cabinet. Large economic forces favoured Canadian progress, but it is hard to believe they would have worked nearly so well if Sifton had not lashed them onward. He wanted to see the West settled and concentrated on this task with energy and intelligence. First of all he cleared away a lot of obstacles to western settlement. He ended the policy of giving land grants to railway companies and cut through quantities of red tape that had made slow work of the business of granting any particular piece of land to a prospective settler. Then he turned to the business of

attracting immigrants to Canada. Sifton wanted to fill the
Canadian West with good farmers and he didn't care at all
where they came from. Canadian immigration agencies were
opened in hopeful locations—in Britain, the United States,
and Austria-Hungary in particular. He did all in his power to
bring the Canadian West to the attention of the world. Parties
of American newspaper editors and their wives were brought
north to see its possibilities for themselves; successful farmers
of British birth were sent back to Great Britain to testify to
the great possibilities of western Canada; immigration officers
tried to persuade French Canadians in New England to emi-
grate to western Canada; and Sifton's men discovered in
Austria-Hungary a rich source of emigrants from its overpop-
ulated rural areas.

The good news about this "last best West" fell on ears
willing to hear. The trickle of immigrants became a stream,
and finally a mighty flood. In 1896 there were 20,000; in
1906 190,000; and on and up the figures went. Western
Canada grew spectacularly during the Laurier years: between
1896 and 1911 over a million people settled on the prairies.

Meanwhile the United States became a far less interesting
neighbour. Annexationism, so common in the late 1880s
when Canadians were despondent about their future, ceased
absolutely to be a topic. The Liberals had abandoned Unrestricted Reciprocity shortly after the elections of 1891; after
1896 they stopped trying to lower the customs barriers
between the two countries, for the Americans made it clear
that the only kind of tariffs they wanted were higher ones.
The Liberals satisfied themselves with the low tariffs to Great
Britain embodied in the Imperial Preference, and Canadians
stopped being preoccupied by the idea of reciprocity with
the United States.

Canadians and Americans still had a lot of subjects to talk about, however. Canada was enough of a colony to have its foreign relations managed under British auspices, but Canadian representatives were increasingly involved in discussions and their agreement was essential to settlement. Nowhere were Canadians more anxious to make their own arrangements than in their dealings with the United States. This was made clear at a meeting of the Joint High Commission in 1898 when the talks produced some disagreement. "The stumbling-block", wrote Laurier, "was the Alaska boundary." The Americans had bought Alaska from Russia in 1867, and for years the boundary of Alaska had crept without much debate far down the coast of British Columbia, making it impossible for British Columbians to get to the Yukon the only easy way—by sea. There had been some discussion before 1898 about where the real boundary of Alaska lay, but in that year, and for some time after, the question became urgent since the Yukon was swarming with goldminers. The merchants of Seattle and the merchants of Vancouver were determined to supply the miners with equipment, and each group wanted to exclude the other. The question was, who would succeed? Did Canadians rightly claim possession of land at the head of the Lynn Inlet, which would give them access to the Yukon?

Negotiations went on for four years to discover a reasonable judicial settlement of the question. At least that is what the Canadians said they wanted. The Americans were not inclined to admit there was a question. President Theodore Roosevelt declared: "The claim of the Canadians for access to deep water along any part of the Alaskan coast is just exactly as indefensible as if they should now suddenly claim the island of Nantucket." In 1902 Laurier yielded to British pressure for settlement—the British were anxious to cultivate Anglo-American friendship. Perhaps too he realized that Americans would accept no other form of settlement than the one they proposed: a commission of "six impartial jurists", three to be chosen by each of the two participants to the dispute. Maybe the end was implicit in this beginning, for at least two of the American choices were known partisans. One, indeed, was a senator from Washington, the state most opposed to Canadian claims. The British choices were less flagrantly political: two were Canadian and the third—Lord Alverstone, Chief Justice of England—was more indisputably impartial. Alverstone, flanked by eager partisans on the commission, was very much alone. Americans and Canadians presented their cases to the Commission: each was determined not to lose, or at least the Canadians were determined not to lose everything. What Canadians wanted was an outlet to the sea; what they got were two irrelevant islands at the mouth of the Portland Channel. The islands were meant to soothe; instead they enraged the Canadian commissioners, furious with Lord Alverstone for largely accepting the American case. The two Canadians refused to sign the award, declaring that it was a political, not a judicial, decision. All Canada shared their rage. Laurier expressed the national frustration clearly: "What were we to do? I have often regretted . . . never more than on the present occasion, that we are living beside a great neighbour who, I believe I can say without being deemed unfriendly to them, are very grasping in their national actions and who are determined on every occasion to get the best in any agreement which they make. I have often regretted also that while they are a great and powerful nation, we are only a small colony—a growing colony, but still a colony. I have often regretted also that we have not in our hands the treaty-making power which would enable us to dispose of our own affairs. But in this matter we are dealing with a position that was forced upon us—we have not the treaty-making power."

The feverish interest in the Yukon declined; soon Dawson City would be a ghost town. All the same it is important to remember Canadians' outrage at the decision of the Alaska Boundary Commission. It was directed against the Americans, but especially against Great Britain for its betrayal of Canadian interests, and showed that the colony of Canada was beginning to want nationhood and was optimistic enough to think it could deal better with the United States without the help of Great Britain.

After the Alaska Boundary dispute, Canadians soon got back to their major preoccupation at this time: economic development. In particular they got back to railway building. As immigrants began to pour into Canada and wheat production in the West soared upwards, as trade and business in all parts of Canada expanded, the demand for more and more railways became urgent. The Canadian Pacific Railway, which had seemed almost more than sufficient when it was finished in 1885, was no longer adequate. In 1901 and 1902 it was unable to transport all the wheat produced in western Canada. Western farmers urged that a second transcontinental be built at once.

Laurier and the Liberals were eager to meet the demand for more railways in general and a new transcontinental in particular. In 1902 they were approached by the Grand Trunk Railway Company, which half a century earlier had been the first to build a line across the old province of Canada. It had long had a reputation for caution that its ambitious new American manager, C. M. Hays, meant to

change. He asked the Liberal government for help in building
west from North Bay, Ontario, to the Pacific. The Grand
Trunk was strongly organized in central Canada, but its
eastern terminal was in Portland, Maine. To the nationalistic
Liberals this did not seem a satisfactory conclusion for a
Canadian railway. As Laurier observed: "I have found the
best and most effective way to maintain friendship with our
American neighbours is to be absolutely independent of
them."

The Grand Trunk was not the only ambitious railway
company. In the West the Canadian Northern was rapidly
emerging out of a growing collection of short lines; already in
1902 it had reached Port Arthur, and was eager to press east
as well as west to the Pacific coast. Donald Mann and William
Mackenzie, its promoters, had a real understanding of what
was needed in the West: cheap lines and lots of them.

The sensible way to provide Canada with a second transcontinental was for the Liberal government to help the Canadian Northern complete a main line from Port Arthur to the
Pacific coast, and for the Grand Trunk to build east from
Port Arthur to Quebec. Everyone saw this clearly enough
afterwards, and even at the time there were those like Clifford Sifton in the Liberal cabinet and Robert Borden, leader
of the Conservative party, who favoured this solution. Laurier himself tried to bring the Canadian Northern and Grand
Trunk together; but the ambitions of Mann on the one hand,
and Hays on the other, were too large for them to find
happiness in just half a transcontinental each. Sifton thought
the two companies "should be required" to come together;
but he was away in England superintending the presentation
of Canada's case before the Alaska Boundary Commission.
Laurier tried to use persuasion, but he failed to bring the two

companies together. The government eventually reached an agreement with the Grand Trunk to build a transcontinental following an all-Canadian route. By its terms the Grand Trunk agreed to build a line from Winnipeg to the Pacific coast, aided partly by government guaranteed bonds; the government of Canada itself was to build a line from Winnipeg to Moncton, New Brunswick, to be leased when it was finished to the Grand Trunk Pacific Company. The Winnipeg-to-Moncton section, called the National Transcontinental, was a politician's dream: the Maritimes, inclined to feel neglected, were included; and Quebec—interested in colonizing northern Quebec, not western Canada—could see in the National Transcontinental a particularly elegant colonization railway. But it was a businessman's nightmare; it made little sense to build a first-class railway through the wilderness of northern Ontario and Quebec to run east into New Brunswick where it would compete with the Intercolonial, a railway that seldom made any money. Laurier was a careful politician, however, not a careful businessman. He won support for his all-Canadian route from all of Canada: no region had cause to be jealous of any other.

Laurier himself presented the agreement for the new transcontinental to the House of Commons. He made a rather florid speech on this occasion, which suited the grandiose plan. The all-Canadian transcontinental won support from the Canadian people in the general elections of 1904. To a warmly enthusiastic audience in Toronto he said: "You cheer me but you do not vote for me." But Toronto wasn't Canada. Most Canadians agreed with Laurier when he said: "The twentieth century shall be the century of Canada and of Canadian development!" They voted overwhelmingly for Laurier and prosperity.

5

Decline and Fall

In 1904 Laurier's prestige was at its peak. Under his leadership the Liberals won a majority of 74 seats in the election of that year. Most important to Laurier was his success in improving relations between English- and French-speaking Canadians. In dealing with the Manitoba schools controversy and the question of Canadian participation in the Boer War, Laurier had been able to arrange a compromise that satisfied all but the most exacting members of both races. But a politician's success is fragile: it depends more on his ability to settle the next crisis than the last one. Laurier was trailing clouds of glory, but his progress was being followed with acute interest by a number of critics.

In Quebec, for example, the Liberal party won 54 seats and seemed to have no serious enemies—certainly not the Conservatives, for they had never recovered from the loss of the Chapleau *Bleus*. But underneath the placid surface there were stirrings. For one thing Bourassa did not return to the Liberal party. He remained in the House of Commons as an Independent and more and more his thoughts turned to the great problem of French-Canadian survival. He did not care for the new industrialism that was transforming Quebec from a rural into an urban economy, controlled by English and American capitalists; and he feared the floods of immigrants

—aliens who would soon join the English and make the
French a still smaller minority, perhaps destroying forever
Bourassa's idea of Canada as a bicultural nation, a country
where "there are neither conquerors nor conquered ones",
where "there are two partners whose partnership was entered
into upon fair and well-defined lines." The newcomers would
not understand all this: they would spoil, not make, the
Canada Bourassa had in mind.

Bourassa was not alone in his concern; he soon became the
idol of the young students at the classical colleges and was
fondly regarded by their teachers as well. Very largely inspired by him were two small movements begun in 1903. The
object of the first, La Ligue Nationaliste, was Canadian
autonomy within the Empire, and provincial autonomy within Canada: its members seemed to be Canadian nationalists
but were entirely French in their sharp hostility to English-
Canadian imperialism. The second group, L'Association Ca-
tholique de la Jeunesse Canadienne-Française, celebrated
French-Canadian nationality and was prepared to defend it
ardently. Supporting it were important Roman Catholic clerics like the abbé Lionel Groulx, who emphasized the central
place of Roman Catholicism in French-Canadian nationality.
Bourassa entirely agreed with them. At first the movements
were so small as to be nearly invisible; only politicians as
sensitive as Laurier worried when Bourassa referred to "my
young army".

Among the members of the army was the son of Emilie
Lavergne, who admired not only Laurier but England and all
things English. Armand's response to all this domestic Eng-
lishness was to turn into a thorough French-Canadian nationalist. He was an enthusiast for old Quebec, charmed by its
buildings, its small industries, the sweetness and simplicity of

life in its small towns, and he would have been glad to "throw the whole of the English population into the St Lawrence". In 1904, at the age of twenty-four, he was elected to parliament as a Liberal, even though he refused to pledge his loyalty .to the party. Soon he was the warmest of Bourassa's allies. These two watched carefully to see how well Laurier defended French-Canadian interests, and it was not long before their worst expectations were realized.

After the election of 1904 the Liberals turned at once to the business of creating two new provinces, Alberta and Saskatchewan, out of the North West Territories. The new provinces were a clear testimony to the success of the Liberal policies of development, but their creation was to injure gravely Laurier's policy of conciliation between French and English. Not surprisingly, the trouble centred on the question of education: What kind of rights should religious minorities have in the new provinces? Laurier, as he so often declared, really was intellectually an English liberal; and in setting up the provinces of Alberta and Saskatchewan in 1905 he wanted to assure to the Roman Catholic minority some freedom to educate their own children in their own way, no matter what the majority in those provinces wanted, then or ever. He was not wedded to any one educational system but he did want to avoid leaving the minority deprived and resentful. The bills creating Alberta and Saskatchewan provided the minority with the right to establish their own schools and share in public funds for their support. In parliament Laurier emphasized the value of religion in education, contrasting Canada with the United States: "When I compare the status of the two nations, when I think upon their future, when I observe the social condition of civil society in each of them and when I observe in this country of ours a total absence of lynchings and an almost total absence of divorces and murders, for my part I thank Heaven that we are living in a country where the young children of the land are taught Christian morals and Christian dogmas."

The comparison cut very little ice with Clifford Sifton, the strongest Liberal in the West. He thought the people who actually lived in the West ought to decide what kind of school system they wanted; he strongly resented any effort to limit the freedom of the majority who lived in Alberta and Saskatchewan. He had no sympathy with any separate-school system and thought Laurier supported the creation of such a system to please the Roman Catholics of Quebec.

Sifton did not stand alone. The air, particularly in Ontario, was hot with objections from Liberals and Conservatives. Laurier's early admirer, John Willison, departed from him on the matter of religion in the schools. He thought education ought to be controlled by the state, not by any church. As to the question of Roman-Catholic control, his instincts were all Protestant: "The hierarchy have never touched education except to check, embarrass, and prevent the free play of human intelligence." Laurier was very depressed by the opposition of English-speaking Canadians to what seemed to him an entirely liberal arrangement. He thought seriously of resigning; but then, to prevent an even greater clash between Protestants and Roman Catholics, he decided to yield to Sifton, who had resigned from the cabinet, and also to Fielding, who was on the verge of resigning. What Sifton proposed was that the rights of minorities as defined in 1901 by the Assembly of the North West Territories be assured; these rights were very few indeed, consisting chiefly in allowing religion to be taught in the last half-hour of the school day. Laurier accepted Sifton's compromise proposal—and

Quebec took note of his "giving in" once more to English-speaking Canada. His prestige dropped considerably in his own province. Bourassa was glum about this further retreat from his ideal of an Anglo-French nation in which each partner had equal rights. There was no question of giving language rights to the tiny French-Canadian population, and now even their religious education was undermined. In the House he said: "I regret every time I go back to my province . . . to find developing that feeling that Canada is not Canada for all Canadians. We are bound to come to the conclusion that Quebec is our only country because we have no liberty elsewhere." Bourassa referred bitterly to the newcomers to the West as "those thousands of strangers who have contributed nothing to the building of the country, who have made no sacrifices to the cause of national unity, and who, if we ever had to pass through some fearsome test, would not associate themselves with it."

Laurier, the serene and reasonable liberal, did not share the deep fear of French Canadians that they would be swamped by immigration. He did not think they should sit in their fortress of Quebec, brooding about the aliens who surrounded them: "I should like to see . . . a good number of young men of talent, lawyers or doctors, go and pitch their tents in the English provinces and there make a good position for themselves by their work and virtue. Nothing would contribute more to destroy the national barriers of prejudice and to create precious sympathy for us in all parts of Canada." On the other hand, Laurier could not understand the anxiety of Protestant Canada about allowing to Roman-Catholic minorities in their midst the same kind of control over education that the Protestant minority in Quebec possessed. French Canadians were illiberal about immigration. English Cana-

Henri Bourassa, about 1910

dians were illiberal about separate schools. Both, it seemed, lacked confidence in their ability to survive. In the West particularly, English-speaking Canadians were determined to have a single state-controlled system: it seemed the only possible way to unite a population of widely differing origins. Laurier was a self-assured liberal; he did not see why the English-speaking majority should find minority rights so hard to concede in the schools, nor did he think it possible that French Canadians would be lost in a sea of immigrants.

Clifford Sifton did not return to the Liberal cabinet even after the acceptance of his revision to the separate-school clause in the acts creating Alberta and Saskatchewan. He was not the first strong cabinet minister that Laurier had lost. Through the years the distinguished abilities that had characterized Laurier's first cabinet in 1896 had gradually fallen away. The loss of some was inevitable. Oliver Mowat was an old man and his health was precarious, so that it was no surprise when he resigned in 1897 to become Lieutenant-Governor of Ontario. The case of Israel Tarte in 1902 was far different: his crusade for higher tariffs ended in his dismissal from the cabinet. Laurier lost his Minister of Railways, A.G. Blair, who opposed the agreement with the Grand Trunk to build the transcontinental. The Liberal party had been growing steadily weaker in Ontario and he did not find strong cabinet replacements in that province. It remained strong in Quebec, but there he had lost the most promising of prospective cabinet ministers, Henri Bourassa. Bourassa never returned to the Liberal party after his resignation in 1899; in 1908 he resigned from the House of Commons in order to run for election to the Quebec Assembly. Laurier's farewell message was wonderfully precise: "I regret your going. We need a man like you at Ottawa, though I should not want two." Bourassa, who was to say many exceptionally bitter things about Laurier and campaign furiously against him, later wrote: "Although I fought him because of differences of principle, I loved him all my life and he knew that."

The level of the Liberal cabinet sank steadily. Instead of having to deal with the undisciplined enthusiasm of Israel Tarte, Laurier now had to cope with the weakness of Henry R. Emmerson, Minister of Railways, who was a heavy drinker. At Laurier's insistence he took the pledge in 1906: "I hereby pledge my word to Sir Wilfrid Laurier that I will never again taste wine, beer or any other mixed or intoxicating liquors, in token of which engagement I place in Sir W.L.'s hands my resignation as a member of the cabinet and Minister of Railways with the date in blank, leaving it to him to fill in the blank and act upon it should I fail in my promise. *Henry R. Emmerson.*" A year later Laurier filled in the blank and Emmerson left the cabinet.

Graft and corruption flourished in these easy times when there were a great many government contracts, and large profits to be made from winning them. The depths to which the once-virtuous Liberals had sunk were explored in a number of parliamentary sessions after 1906. The Department of the Interior attracted a good deal of criticism. It was widely believed that the policies of this department had not only developed Canada but made the fortunes of a number of favoured individuals. For instance, critics charged that timber and grazing contracts had benefited hugely their lucky recipients, one of whom, T.A. Burrows, was a brother-in-law of Sifton's. Sifton rebutted all the charges with his customary vigour. Among other things, he pointed out that his brother-in-law had been a lumberman for a long time and earlier had won timber contracts from the Conservative government. His defence was good but fell short of carrying conviction.

The Department of the Interior was not the only alleged sinner; indeed, investigation revealed a good deal of graft in the Marine and Fisheries Department. In 1906 Charles Hyman, the new Minister of Public Works, had to resign because of charges of corrupt electioneering. But corruption did not begin and end with the cabinet. M.P.s tried very hard to get appointed as judges or senators, or even to win knighthoods. They promised, and very often provided, favours for their constituencies in the form of bridges, customs houses, railway subsidies, and jobs. After his election victory in 1896, Laurier received this complaint from a Quebec follower: "If anyone had told me when I was fighting the battles of Liberalism in my county, striving without fear of attack or hope of favour to advance the cause of the people, determined that no designing cleric and no corrupt politician would be allowed to shackle our noble country—if anyone had told me that six months after you took office I would still be without a job, I would not have believed him." The pressure of office-seekers never diminished.

Laurier, who was not involved in the numerous scandals, was anxious to work for the reformation of his party. The Liberal government moved to check some of the evils of party patronage by creating in 1907 a Civil Service Commission: that is to say, they hoped to build a Civil Service staffed by people of tested ability, not simply those able to wangle a recommendation from their M.P. In this same year Laurier tried to get two strong men back in his cabinet: Bourassa and Sifton. He failed with both. Sifton's terms were high: he wanted to bring three sympathizers with him into the cabinet to strengthen his influence. Sifton was a man of strong will who saw this same quality in Laurier. "Despite his courtesy

and gracious charm," Sifton declared, Laurier was "a master-
ful man set on having his own way, and equally resolute that
his colleagues shall not have their way unless this is quite
agreeable to him." Laurier refused to meet Sifton's terms,
plaintively urging the impossibility of getting rid of elderly
colleagues who had been loyal in hard times. Perhaps his
refusal simply meant that he had no desire to hand over the
mastery of the cabinet to Sifton; perhaps also Laurier no
longer cared to be surrounded by forceful individuals, brist-
ling with ego and energy.

It was a sadly tarnished Liberal party that approached the
elections of 1908. Resignations of erring Liberals had been
accepted and reforms in administration had been made, but
reputations are more easily lost than regained: the Liberals
were clearly not as virtuous as they had once claimed to be.
There were exceptions, and Laurier was the chief of these:
his great name and good reputation were to do much to carry
the Liberals once again to victory in 1908. Continuing prosperity was also to help: immigrants still poured into western
Canada, railways shot out in all directions, eastern industry
grew to meet the demands of the new West. It all seemed
miraculous to Canadians at the time, and it is easy to understand their rather stunned delight. Here is a contemporary
account of the growth of North Battleford, Saskatchewan. It
was "ushered into existence in June 1905 with one house to
its credit. Six months later it had a population of five
hundred. Farm property at $6.00 an acre in June now be-
came city lots at $10.00 per foot. It now [1906] has shops
of every kind, a large hotel and four churches. It is difficult
to find a resident who does not believe that nearly the same
ratio of increase in size and prosperity is to be maintained
indefinitely. The spirit of optimism is abroad in the land;

Laurier and his public
Above: *Campaigning in the federal elections of 1908*
Below: *Receiving an address at Mission City, 16 August 1910*

there are a hundred more bustling little cities on the mainline and branches of the railway, all growing rapidly."

The Liberals appropriated this prosperity as their own achievement; they could also claim Laurier's continued success in maintaining Canada's position of quasi-independence within the Empire. At the Colonial Conference in 1907 Laurier had again opposed plans to centralize the running of the Empire; he was a supporter of the resolution to call future meetings Imperial Conferences, to emphasize the equality of the self-governing dominions with the British government. "We are all His Majesty's governments," Laurier insisted. But the cause of imperial unity had lost a good deal of ground in Great Britain after the Liberals took office there in 1906, and in Canada it temporarily ceased to excite much enthusiasm among English-speaking Canadians, though French Canadians still took a nervous interest in imperial questions and were pleased by Laurier's firm insistence on Canadian autonomy.

In the election campaign of 1908 the Liberals could stress the progress Canada had made under their government. While Laurier admitted that corruption had occurred and declared that the Liberals were reforming abuses and would continue to reform them, he kept their positive achievements well before his audiences: "We have been twelve years in office and these years will be remembered in the history of Canada. In them Canada has been lifted from the humble position of a colony to that of a nation. In 1896 Canada was a mere colony, hardly known in the United States or Europe. In 1908 Canada has become a star to which is directed the gaze of the civilized world. This is what we have done."

Sifton put the Liberals' claims for re-election in a more down-to-earth way: "The policy of Sir Wilfrid Laurier represents the completion of the National Transcontinental, the building of a line of railway to Hudson's Bay, and the development of the national resources. Negation, criticism, and scandal are offered by the opposition."

Canadians were persuaded to "Let Laurier Finish His Work" and the Liberals won an overall majority of 47 seats; but the response was not so enthusiastic as it once had been. The Liberals got a majority of only 25,000 out of the total popular vote of one and a half million.

Laurier was depressed by the results and considered resigning. Indeed, he wrote a letter of resignation, but Fielding, his prospective successor, dissuaded him, and the Liberal government went on much as before. It was not noticeably transformed by new blood, though reforms had purified it somewhat: there was less talk of scandal in the new parliament. In a quiet way the new government made a number of intelligent changes. Laurier, agreeing with a motion of Borden's, established a Committee of Natural Resources to check the wastage of Canada's fisheries, mines, forests and water by heedless private interests. In Sifton he found a capable chairman for the committee, and so a small beginning was made to solve a growing problem: people at the time thought of resources as inexhaustible. Another useful innovation was the establishment of the Department of External Affairs in 1909. "The foreign affairs with which Canada has to deal", said Laurier, "are becoming of such absorbing moment as to necessitate special machinery." The beginning was so modest that not even Canadian imperialists were alarmed, but perhaps nationalists could see that at least Canada was equipping itself to take the management of its affairs into its own hands.

Railways and wheat production were not the only things

that shot ahead in the golden Laurier years. In another field too Laurier and the Liberals were showing an alertness to developments that had scarcely yet captured the popular imagination. In central Canada manufacturing grew strikingly. Pulp and paper industries gave life to marginal farming areas, and cities like Montreal and Toronto grew apace. So did the working class in these and other cities. It grew in numbers, however, not necessarily in prosperity. The dreadful slums of Montreal had a death-rate of thirty-four for every thousand people, and the death-rate in the city as a whole was higher than that in London or Paris or New York.

The miseries of the city poor aroused the interest of Mackenzie King, grandson of the rebel leader William Lyon Mackenzie and proud of it. His humanitarianism was tempered by a strong ambition to succeed. Even as a university undergraduate he busily concerned himself with the poor and unfortunate—visiting children in hospital, attempting to reform prostitutes, helping to organize an association for newsboys. King discovered early the problems of urban workers in Canada. He brought to the attention of William Mulock, the Postmaster General, the awful conditions under which uniforms were made for the federal government. Mulock promptly got King to help draw up regulations that would end bad working conditions in any company wanting to make postal uniforms for the government, and Laurier made the regulations apply to all government contracts. After this small beginning, King joined the federal civil service. In 1900, not yet twenty-six, he became editor of the new government publication, the *Labour Gazette.* Soon he was made deputy minister of the newly created Labour Department, established under the wing of the Postmaster General; in 1909 he became minister of the now-independent Department of Labour. In addition to organizing his department, King did useful work in settling strikes where the disputants chose to call in a federal conciliator. But his work was limited, partly because the federal government had so much less power than the provinces where labour matters were concerned and partly because the plight of the working classes did not catch the imagination of the Canadian public—farmers and farmers' problems loomed so much larger. Laurier's interest was similarly lukewarm. He recognized King's ability, charmed him, encouraged him warmly and vaguely; but Laurier's interest in King and labour remained peripheral to his main preoccupation: the promotion of good relations between French and English Canadians. If he had a thought to spare it was for those struggling wheat farmers in western Canada. Maybe the urban masses didn't seem real to the nineteenth-century liberal from small-town Quebec.

Laurier remained clear-sighted in his judgement of himself and his aging associates. As he wrote to a fellow Liberal who lost a nomination in 1909: "You forget that you, and I as well, are no longer as young as we used to be when we campaigned together. The young are coming up and taking the place of the old fellows. That is what has happened to you in your county, and that is what will happen to me before long in Canada. Let us submit with good grace to the inevitable." That Laurier's cabinet was not getting any younger struck Mackenzie King forcibly too, for he noted in his diary the many times he found ministers asleep during cabinet meetings. Laurier remained awake, however. His physical energy was lessening but he meant to use it to the very end, even though there were moments of depression and times when he thought of resignation.

Laurier needed his clear mind and strong will to settle a

new dispute between English- and French-speaking Canadians that developed after 1909 and threatened Canadian unity quite as much as any of the earlier conflicts that Laurier had solved by compromise. It concerned the establishment of a Canadian navy, which had never seemed a very urgent necessity for Canadians, preoccupied with the development of the interior of Canada and accustomed to the protection of the British navy. At the Colonial Conference of 1902 Laurier was approached by Chamberlain for contributions to the imperial navy, from which Canada benefited but for which it paid nothing. He rejected the proposal, saying that Canada was thinking of establishing its own navy. Nothing more was heard about the Canadian navy until 1909. In that year the First Lord of the Admiralty alarmed his own country and much of the Empire by declaring that Britain would shortly lose her naval supremacy to Germany, for Germans were building more battleships than the British.

Imperial passions had seemed to die down in English Canada after the Boer war, but they did not really disappear. Popular songs like "Rule Britannia" and "Soldiers of the Queen" helped see to that. And in Ontario at any rate, schoolchildren were brought up on English patriotic poems and tales of English heroism. The imperial adventures described in G.A. Henty's novels were popular with both boys and adults. The pluck and daring of his heroes were admired by boys, while the fact that in ninety books they "nothing sordid did or mean" recommended the Henty books to adults.

The British Empire was a heroic cause to a great many English Canadians and in 1909 they felt that any real threat to its security had to be combatted. Laurier also attached a good deal of importance to the British Empire. He declared in parliament: "If the day should come when the supremacy of Britain on the high seas will be challenged, it will be the duty of all the daughter nations to close around the old Motherland and make a rampart about her to ward off any attack." He believed that "the salvation of England is the salvation of our own country, that therein lies the guaranty of our civil and religious freedom and everything we value in this life." He agreed with Conservatives Borden and Foster, who proposed that "a Canadian naval force of our own" be organized at once and in co-operation with the imperial navy. The Liberal government had plans for a Canadian navy drawn up by the British Admiralty, and in January 1910 Laurier introduced a Naval Service Bill that provided for the establishment of a permanent naval force to be staffed by volunteers, controlled by the Canadian government. Five cruisers and six destroyers were to be built for $11,000,000; and the annual cost of the navy was expected to be about $3,000,000. The bill seemed impeccably moderate, well calculated to win the support of reasonable men like the leader of the Conservative party, Robert Borden, for it strengthened the imperial navy by taking over Canadian responsibilities, and it strengthened Great Britain in any emergency that might occur, for then the Canadian government would send its navy to its support. All the same it was the Canadian government that would decide exactly what constituted an emergency, a point Laurier made extremely clear: "If England is at war, we are at war and liable to attack. I do not say that we shall always be attacked, neither do I say that we would take part in all the wars of England. That is a matter that must be guided by circumstances, upon which the Canadian parliament will have to pronounce, and will have to decide in its own best judgement." What could be fairer than that? The Laurier policy took into account both Canada's independence and the importance of her connection with Great Britain.

Although Robert Borden had felt in 1909 that "our best course was to establish a Canadian naval force", it was soon obvious that much of his party did not agree with him. Imperialist Conservatives rejected the idea of a Canadian navy—"a tin-pot navy", said Manitoba's Conservative Premier Roblin—and urged that Canada should help at once and in the future to maintain the strength of the imperial navy. Conservatives in Quebec were equally opposed to a Canadian navy, but for quite different reasons. They shared Bourassa's deep hostility to involvement in British imperialist wars that really were of no concern to Canada. As for Bourassa himself, once Laurier's naval policy was announced, he spoke against it. He felt there ought to be a plebiscite on the creation of a navy and he worked strongly on French-Canadian apprehensions that a Canadian navy would facilitate Canadian involvement in British wars. He argued that the British maintained a great navy to defend not Canada but rather their worldwide commercial interests. Canada was threatened only by Great Britain and the United States, and the United States would allow no foreign power to trifle with Canada, for Canada was on her doorstep. As for the British navy, it offered no protection at all to Canadians against the United States, so why should Canadians strengthen it?

Bourassa attracted support in Quebec not only from the Conservatives but also in the classical colleges, from teachers and students alike. They subscribed to his new newspaper, *Le Devoir,* founded in January 1910; indeed, *Le Devoir* was often the only newspaper read by clergy, teachers, and students and it is easy to see why. Right from the beginning the paper declared its independence and high-minded devotion to duty. In the first issue Bourassa concluded his statement of purpose by saying: "In order to assure the triumph of ideas over appetites, of the public welfare over the party spirit, there is only one way: awaken in the people, and especially in the leading classes, the sentiment of public duty in all its forms: religious duty, national duty, civic duty." In the second issue Bourassa spoke of the "golden clouds" in which Laurier "had veiled the betrayals, weaknesses, and dangers of his policy".

Just how far the fears aroused by Laurier's naval policy had spread was made clear in the Drummond-Arthabaska by-election of 1910, which was necessitated by the appointment to the senate of Louis Lavergne, uncle of Armand. Bourassa and the federal Conservatives, whose leader in Quebec was F.D. Monk, waged a mighty campaign. They argued that Laurier's navy would lead straight to fighting England's wars and those wars would lead to conscription in Canada. It was reported that men in uniform, who explained that it was necessary to have lists ready when Laurier's Naval Act was put into force, went round to the farmhouses asking the women: "Have you a husband? . . . How many sons? What ages?" The Liberals fought back hard, but all the same their candidate lost. To the tune of "O Canada" the victorious workers sang "O Bourassa". Laurier said: "There are defeats which are more honourable than victories."

Western wheat farmers had become increasingly restless about tariffs and eager for access to American markets. Laurier in particular was well aware of their dissatisfaction. In the summer of 1910 he had made a triumphant tour of the prairie provinces; everywhere he was rapturously welcomed by the new West that had so largely sprung into life under his government. Top-hatted and elegant, the Prime Minister was also humane and responsive. After laying the cornerstone of a university in Saskatoon he told of having a long chat that morning with a voluble newsboy by the name of John Diefenbaker. "Well, Mr Prime Minister," the boy said after a half-hour had passed, "I can't waste any more time. I have to deliver my papers." At a giant outdoor meeting in Edmonton, Laurier paused suddenly in the midst of his speech to regard intently an upper-floor window from which a child leaned too far. "Is that little one safe?" he inquired. The child was retrieved and the speech resumed. Laurier took seriously not only dangling children but also the farmers' deputations that pressed for low-tariff and reciprocity proposals. He was proud of the West and of the work of its people—many of them recent arrivals from Europe—in building it; he was eager to conciliate its grievances and promote its welfare. "I return ten times more Canadian," he said. "I have imbibed the air, spirit and enthusiasm of the West."

Early in 1911 W. S. Fielding, the Minister of Finance, presented to the House of Commons an agreement with the United States for reciprocity in the trading of natural products. It was a triumph, for no Canadian government since 1866 (when the United States had abrogated the treaty of 1854) had been able to cut through the hedge of American tariffs and get at the attractive American market right on Canada's doorstep; and most governments had tried. Actually President Taft, not the Canadian Liberals, had promoted the agreement; but the Liberals had every reason to welcome it and Laurier certainly favoured it.

The agreement allowed farmers or anyone else with natural products to sell in the United States to do so freely, without the impediment of customs duties; but it did not involve

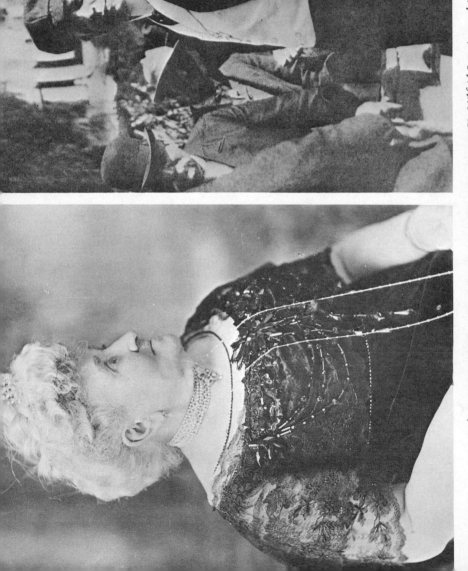

Sir Wilfrid Laurier on his western trip of 1910

Lady Laurier 1911

manufactured products, so small Canadian manufacturers had no reason to fear that Canada would be swamped by the products of large American competitors. The agreement appeared so like a gift horse that the Conservatives scarcely wanted to look it in the mouth. But this mood of dull shock did not last. The Conservatives recovered their spirits as opposition appeared and rose steadily. It came from Canadian manufacturers who feared that reciprocity might be the beginning of even freer trade that in the end would expose them to ruinous competition; it came also from those who wanted to preserve Canadian resources for Canadian use, not encourage their export to the south; and it came with special ardour from the railway builders, who for years had been constructing west-east lines in Canada and who would be ruined if trade suddenly became north-south. "Bust the damn thing!" said CPR's President Van Horne, inelegantly but urgently; and a group of Liberals from Toronto, led by the brilliant organizer Clifford Sifton, got to work to do just that. When the American politician Champ Clark declared he was all for reciprocity "because I hope to see the day when the American flag will float over every square foot of the British North American possessions clear to the North Pole", many Canadians came to believe that the agreement was not a gift horse but a Trojan horse. American enthusiasm for it seemed a decisive reason for rejecting reciprocity, and the Conservatives' slogan, "No Truck Nor Trade with the Yankees", the appropriate reply.

The opposition to the reciprocity bill was such that, shortly after returning in July from the coronation of George V and an Imperial Conference, Laurier decided to appeal to the country in a general election.

Reciprocity did not excite much interest in Quebec—matters of trade seldom did. There the question of the day was the Canadian navy, and opposition was focussed on British, not American, imperialism. In the federal election of 1911 Laurier and the Liberals fought the Conservative-Nationalists led by Bourassa and Monk. With the help of *Le Devoir,* which was circulated everywhere, Bourassa's message that the navy meant conscription did its work. "Bourassa is a man of great ability," Laurier once said, "but his ability is negative and destructive. He will never accomplish anything constructive or of benefit to any cause which he may espouse." In fact he shared with Laurier a great many ideas, among them a belief in Canadian autonomy and a dislike of militarism; but temperamentally the two men were poles apart. Bourassa was ultramontane and carried his religious feelings right into politics; it was natural for him to see in any political quarrel good and evil fighting each other. He once declared: "When Sir Wilfrid Laurier arrives at the gate of Paradise, the first thing he will do is to propose a compromise between God and Satan." Laurier was a born diplomat: in politics he saw the conflict of different points of view, not God and Satan; he had no taste for any kind of holy war, and he had a rational man's respect for differences of opinion.

In 1911 he had not changed but his opponents had grown stronger, as he became aware when he campaigned strenuously for four weeks, addressing more than fifty meetings. In Saint John he said: "I am branded in Quebec as a traitor to the French and in Ontario as a traitor to the English. In Quebec I am branded as a jingo and in Ontario as a separatist. In Quebec I am attacked as an imperialist and in Ontario as an anti-imperialist. I am neither. I am a Canadian. Canada has been the inspiration of my life. I have had before me as a pillar of fire by night and a pillar of cloud by day a policy of true Canadianism, of moderation, of conciliation."

In the election of 1911 Bourassa had the satisfaction of seeing the Liberals lose their big majority in Quebec, for they won only 37 seats. He also contributed to the victory of the Conservative party, a large section of which wanted to form closer ties with the Empire. On the reciprocity issue the Liberals had crushing losses almost everywhere in English-speaking Canada except Alberta and Saskatchewan. But, Laurier said afterwards: "It is the province of Ontario which has defeated us . . . Ontario went solid against us."

The Liberals' program of establishing a Canadian navy and introducing limited free trade with the United States was a reasonable one, but the Liberals themselves were simply unable to calm the anxieties they aroused. French-speaking Canadians did not want to be swept into British imperial causes, and English-speaking Canadians did not want to be absorbed by American capitalism. Or perhaps a great many Canadians were ready and willing to find any reason to vote against the elderly Liberal government. In any event, neither Laurier's great personal charm nor his rational program were able to save the Liberals from defeat in 1911.

Laurier kept his feelings on this occasion to himself. Mackenzie King described him at his last cabinet meeting: "He said while leaning on the back of the chair, raising himself erect & without looking at anyone in particular: 'Well, gentlemen, that is all.' The last three words were less audible than the first two; he turned & walked quickly, head erect and like one victorious to the little door which goes into the anteroom, and without further ceremony he had parted with his colleagues forever."

6
Last Act

There was one loyal Liberal who took the defeat of 1911 philosophically and that was Laurier's wife Zoë, who remarked serenely that it was Providence "which was taking him a little from his country and giving him back to his old wife." Zoë had never much cared for Ottawa because, as she had written to a friend years before, "here I belong to everyone and to no one in particular. I would rather be the wife of a simple avocat in Arthabaska. It was the best time of my life." All the same she had adapted herself to Ottawa with a good deal of success. If she never learned to love official occasions, she certainly knew how to make people comfortable in her house, and did. She made herself comfortable too, living in an amiable clutter of kittens and puppies, enjoying ice cream cones and sharing them with pets on outings in the great chauffeur-driven limousine. Laurier, whose friendship with Emilie Lavergne was a thing of the distant past, found in his wife's companionship relief from the cares of office and support through all difficulties.

In 1911 he was seventy—old enough to retire. He was still very much alive to the charms of life in Arthabaskaville and had long planned to devote his last years to writing books on Canadian history. He did in fact propose his resignation to the party at the beginning of the new parliamentary session, but it was stoutly rejected. He had no regrets, for politics was his life, despite its peculiarly Canadian difficulties. "Our existence as a nation is the most anomalous that has yet existed. We are British subjects but we are an autonomous nation; we are divided into provinces, we are divided into races, and out of these confused elements the man at the head of affairs has to sail the ship onwards." Sailing the ship onwards was what he liked best. "I don't feel ripe for heaven, and at all events I want another tussle with the Tories." His prestige, which the defeat in 1911 could not help but diminish a little, was easily renewed. Bourassa conceded joylessly in 1912 that Laurier was "still the great figure of Canadian politics". He was introduced to an audience of University of Toronto students as "the greatest of all Canadians". (Laurier seized this happy occasion to deliver a bit of advice to his young audience: "If I were your age . . . I would not leave school until I could speak and write in French.")

In parliament Laurier threw himself energetically into the work of restoring Liberal spirits, defending the policies of his late government, and carefully watching the Tories under Prime Minister Borden. In particular he watched to see just what naval policy the Conservatives would devise that would command the support of both wings of the party—the imperialists, eager to strengthen the British navy, and the isolationists of Quebec, who wanted no part in Britain's imperialist wars. There was a long wait. It was well over a year before Borden introduced his naval bill to the House of Commons. Designed to meet the emergency of 1909, when it first became clear that Britain was in danger of losing her naval supremacy to Germany, the bill postponed deciding whether Canada should contribute to imperial defence and so have a voice in imperial policy, as Borden urged, or whether it should develop its own defences and decide for itself when and how much to help Britain in emergencies, as Laurier wanted. Borden brushed these weighty alternatives aside and simply proposed to contribute to the imperial navy 35 million dollars, the cost of three large battleships, so that Britain, not Germany, would rule the waves. A permanent policy, a role for Canada in running the Empire, would be developed later. In the meantime Britain's naval supremacy had to be secured. Monk, the Conservative leader in Quebec, did not agree and resigned.

Laurier attacked the Conservatives vigorously. First of all, he denied that Britain faced an emergency: "There is no immediate danger, there is no prospective danger." We can now see that this view was false, but it was held at the time by many reformers in Britain, who thought that foreign affairs distracted attention and money from the real work to be done at home. More cuttingly, Laurier noted that the Conservatives were willing to send money but not men to England. He made short work of Borden's assurance that the Admiralty would arrange to let Canadians serve on the Canadian ships. Any Canadians likely to apply would be officers trained in the Royal Navy. "Oh, ye Tory jingoes, is that the amount of sacrifice you are prepared to make? You are ready to furnish admirals, rear-admirals, commodores, captains, officers of all grades, plumes, feathers, and gold lace; but you leave it to England to supply the bone and sinews on board those ships. You say that these ships shall bear Canadian names. That will be the only thing Canadian about them. You hire somebody to do your work; in other words, you are ready to do anything except the fighting. Is that, sir, the true policy?" As for Canada's sharing in imperial foreign policy, Laurier doubted whether it was either possible or desirable.

How could the overseas Dominions be consulted about matters that were often highly confidential? What if they disagreed? Anyhow, was Canada interested in all imperial questions—the recent division of Persia? the Afghan boundary question? the sending of German warships to Agadir? Laurier believed that the real basis of the British Empire lay in the freedom of its self-governing dominions. The Crown was the great unifying bond: "Though purely sentimental, [it] has proven itself stronger than armies and navies; has shown itself to be equal to all occasions."

Debate on Borden's naval bill continued for months until finally, in April 1913, the Conservatives introduced closure (i.e. limited the debate) and got the bill through the House of Commons. It was defeated in the Liberal-controlled Senate, however. After years of debate on the naval question, Canada decided in favour of nothing at all: no Canadian navy, no contribution to the imperial navy. Bourassa thought it a "moral triumph without precedent" for the Nationalists of Quebec, and certainly for them it *was* a triumph, though it is hard to see how morality entered into it.

The year before the First World War began the strains of "Rule Britannia" became fainter in Canada. The great questions of the Empire gave way to hard domestic ones as Canadians began to suffer from inflation and economic depression—fever and chills unpleasantly combined. "The question of the day", said Laurier, "is the cost of bread, not of battleships." The Liberals, increasingly combative, did not fail to point out that hard times had come with the Conservatives. They were extremely critical of the Conservatives' agreement to save the Canadian Northern Railway from bankruptcy and help its promoters, Mackenzie and Mann, complete the transcontinental line. Laurier quite agreed that

the transcontinental had to be finished, but he argued that
the Canadian government, having poured much money into
the work, ought to insist on having a good deal more control
over the project. The Liberals fulminated but the Conservative measure passed. The parliamentary session ended and all
went home to enjoy the long hot summer of 1914.

Laurier and his wife went back gratefully to Arthabaska.
In their long life together, surely nothing united them more
strongly than the pleasure they both took in this small town,
surrounded by hills and countryside, dignified by courthouse
and church. Their pleasure grew more intense with the years.
The house, so proudly built in the 1870s, had aged with
them: its bricks were mellow now, and the young trees
around it had grown tall. Zoë, even though her eyesight was
failing badly, was delighted to be in her garden again. Her
husband was also glad to be back: he walked and read and
replied to letters, and in the evenings played bridge with
friends. Much had changed—some of the old faces had disap-
peared and new ones taken their place—but the Lauriers'
style of life had not. They were still surrounded by relations
and by friends and their children. Laurier still delighted in
telling the young ones stories of times past. A couple of years
earlier he had visited the University of Toronto and left the
students there wondering why their professors could not
make history as interesting as Laurier did. For decades he had
been exercising his talent on the youngsters of Arthabaska,
and he continued to do so in 1914.

These were the last days of a century of British peace,
which Canadians had taken so easily for granted. In Europe
there had been no major wars since the time of Napoleon,
though there had been minor conflicts. After the turn of the
century rivalries among the European countries had sharp-

ened, diplomatic crises intensified, and armaments increased. Still, in 1914 the possibility of a full-scale European war seemed unreal—a myth promoted by armament manufacturers. Then came the assassination of the Austrian Archduke Ferdinand at Sarajevo, Serbia, on June 28. This was serious because a quarrel between Austria-Hungary and Serbia could involve Austria's ally Germany, and, on the Serbian side, Russia. Russia in turn was allied with France and France with Britain. Crises were habitual in Europe, however, and the one that resulted from the assassination of the Archduke did not seem important enough to keep Prime Minister Borden from a holiday in Muskoka, where he remained until the end of July. Only then did he return to Ottawa, summon his cabinet ministers, and assure the British government of Canada's support.

Meanwhile the major European powers moved relentlessly but without precise calculation towards war. Germany, already involved on the side of Austria-Hungary against Russia in the dispute over Serbia, hurried on to meet its destiny, which German statesmen hoped was the dominance of Europe. On August 3 Germany declared war on France. On August 4 the British Foreign Secretary informed the German government that Britain would not tolerate an invasion of neutral Belgium, which would be necessary if Germany were to attack France. The Germans were unmoved, and so Britain entered the war to defend the neutrality of Belgium and to honour its alliance with France.

Canadians were remote from the power struggles in Europe and did not follow them closely. Yet Canada had a real interest in how they affected Great Britain, for the imperial connection had always been, psychologically and physically, a defence against absorption by the United States. To defend the Empire was to support Canada's existence as an independent country in North America. In 1914, however, Canadians did not reason in so tough-minded a way; rather they responded with a deep feeling of loyalty to Great Britain. Sentiment, not reason, brought them cheerfully to Britain's support.

At no time were Canadians more sincerely united than in August 1914. Nowhere was this clearer than in the special war session in parliament; and no one expressed Canadian sentiments more clearly than Laurier. "It is our duty," said Laurier, "more pressing upon us than all other duties, at once, on this first day of this extraordinary session of the Canadian parliament, to let Great Britain know, and to let the friends and foes of Great Britain know, that there is in Canada but one mind and one heart, and that all Canadians stand behind the mother country, conscious and proud that she has engaged in this war, not from any selfish motive, for any purpose of aggrandizement, but to maintain untarnished the honour of her name, to fulfil her obligations to her allies, to maintain her treaty obligations, and to save civilization from the unbridled lust of conquest and power." Other points Laurier made are worth noting. Canada was automatically involved in the war—"when Great Britain is at war we are at war"—but it was the nature of the conflict that made Canada's full support especially worthwhile. Britain and the allies were "fighting for freedom against oppression, for democracy against autocracy, for civilization against reversion to that state of barbarism in which the supreme law is the law of might."

In the late summer of 1914 it seemed that all Canada was swept by patriotic enthusiasm. That this exalted mood did not last is not surprising. Canadians talked easily about finding no sacrifice too great, but at the beginning of the war they had very little notion of the meaning of the phrase. They had had no direct experience of war since 1812, and the memory of that experience a century later was pretty dim. The First World War was to change all that, and although it was fought in Europe, the sufferings and heroism it involved burned themselves so deeply into the consciousness of Canadians that November 11, 1918, the day the war ended, is still observed with ceremonies. A certain poignancy clings to the names of those distant battlefields—Ypres in 1915, the Somme in 1916, Vimy Ridge and Passchendaele in 1917—where so many Canadians fought and died. In the end over 400,000 Canadians went overseas and over 60,000 were killed in battle. Unnumbered others returned mutilated in such a way that they were never themselves again. For a country of eight million people, the loss was severe.

Canada contributed munitions and food as well as men to the war effort, on a scale and for a length of time quite beyond the imaginings of prewar politicians. The whole gamut of undertakings required from the federal government a degree of co-ordination and leadership quite beyond its previous experience. As the war went remorselessly and unsuccessfully on, however, and as the casualty lists mounted, people noticed the blunders more than the achievements—the Ross rifles that proved useless in battle, the bad boots, the dud shells. Profiteers and rumours of war-profiteers grew in numbers as wartime industries appeared out of nowhere. Hard-faced men who did well out of the war disturbed ordinary citizens scanning the casualty lists anxiously, coping with inflation painfully, harvesting bumper crops without help. Canada's economy flourished because of the war, but prosperity was clouded by resentments and miseries.

With a sad inevitability the resentments to which the

strains of war gave rise were harshly reflected in the relations
between English- and French-speaking Canadians. Laurier's
proud claim that "there is in Canada but one mind and one
heart" soon ceased to be true. The French Canadians did not
possess the close emotional attachment felt for Great Britain
by most English-speaking Canadians, and their connection
with modern France, in which the yeast of revolution still
worked, was scarcely intimate. They were loyal to Britain
within reason, but their first preoccupation tended to be
French Canada's struggle to survive within North America.
Borden's Conservative government was not responsible for
the fact that enthusiasm for the war effort did not run
terribly deep in Quebec, but it was responsible for helping to
destroy, by a series of blunders, what support there was.
Borden himself was an open and honourable person, totally
without malice; but as a Nova Scotian he had little direct
knowledge of French Canadians, and his cabinet ministers did
not enlighten him. The Nationalists who had joined the
Conservatives in 1911 to oppose Laurier's Naval Act were not
strong men either in the Conservative government or in
Quebec: they had little influence with Borden and did not
carry much weight in Quebec. In 1911 they had opposed
taking part in Britain's wars; their support of the war when it
began was not convincing.

More spectacular than any of the former Nationalists in
the cabinet was the Minister of Militia, Sam Hughes, a man of
confidence and energy but without sense or sensitivity. The
energy he displayed in scrambling together the first Canadian
contingent impressed many English-speaking Canadians. It
sailed from Canada as early as October 3, 1914, in such a
state of disorganization that it took nine days after the
contingent arrived in England to sort out the muddle of men,

horses, and equipment—some of it useless. Borden later wrote that half the time Hughes was a useful colleague but often "his conduct and speech were so eccentric as to justify the conclusion that his mind was unbalanced." He fired Hughes in 1916, but not before his minister's erratic behaviour had had some disastrous effects among French Canadians. They saw in the Orangeman Hughes a particular enemy, and not without reason. At the beginning of the war he ignored the old militia units and formed new battalions in which no attention was paid to the language of the recruits. It took a good deal of pressure to get even one French-Canadian regiment formed in 1914. For a long time it was the only one: French Canadians were not enthusiastic about enrolling in an English army. The general in charge of the Quebec districts could not speak French and—a quite unforgivable affront—the chief recruiting agent in the Montreal area was a former Methodist clergyman. Altogether the Borden government was neither careful nor sensitive in its dealings with the French Canadians during the early war years.

Laurier and the Liberals never wavered in their support of the war effort, but they were severely tried by what they regarded as major Conservative blunders in the conduct of the war. The Liberals itched to take matters into their own hands, though Laurier opposed a wartime election: "I do not care, for my part, so long as the war lasts, to open the portals of office with that bloody key." By now an elderly man whose physical strength was waning, Laurier threw himself into a busy schedule of recruiting speeches in which he emphasized the greatness of the allied cause—"for freedom and against autocracy, for democrary against autocracy"—and the fact that there was no compulsion to serve. "If some Canadians were frightened by the monster of conscription in

Sir Wilfrid Laurier at the time of the Liberal campaign in

the past, they must now recognize that this monster was a myth." He pleaded with French Canadians to enlist: "I would not have my compatriots of French speech take an attitude different from the attitude of my fellow-countrymen of English speech on this question." In September 1915 Laurier collapsed at a recruiting rally in Napanee and was taken to hospital; he did not return to his war effort until October.

French Canadians heeded Laurier's words and enlisted, but not in great numbers. They no longer listened to Laurier alone; he was not the undisputed *chef,* nor was the war in Europe their main concern. Bourassa and the Nationalists helped see to that. The Ontario school question became the central preoccupation of French Canadians. For Nationalists like Lavergne it had been the primary issue from the very first day of the war, when he said, "If we are asked to go and fight for England . . . we reply—'Let us have our schools.' "

The Ontario school question had its small beginnings shortly after the turn of the century in Ottawa, where Irish and French Catholics struggled for control over the separate-school system. Soon the struggle broadened and deepened: the big question became the place of the French language in the Ontario school system. Investigations into the schools attended by French-speaking students revealed that all too often English was not taught much or well, and that very often the overall quality of the education left much to be desired. The French minority in Ontario was growing rapidly and was much inclined to press for recognition of the right to education in the French language, for it believed that French was a legal, official language in Ontario as it was in Quebec. English-speaking people in Ontario were quick to deny this—sometimes fervently, like the Irish Roman Catholic

Bishop of London, Ontario, and the increasingly aroused anti-Catholic Orange Order. Not everyone was excited over the issue, but there was a deep-seated belief that Ontario was "an English province": on this point provincial Liberals did not differ much from the Conservatives who formed the government of Ontario. Opposition to the Department of Education's "Regulation 17", which limited the use of French as a language of instruction to the early grades in Ontario schools, came from the French-Canadian minority in Ontario and from the Nationalists of Quebec. It was sharp before the war but rose steadily to a climax in 1916. In Quebec the campaign to aid the French-Canadian minority in Ontario seemed much more important than winning the war in Europe. Bourassa wrote in *Le Devoir:* "In the name of religion, liberty, and faithfulness to the British flag, the French Canadians are enjoined to fight the Prussians of Europe. Shall we let the Prussians of Ontario impose their domination like masters, in the very heart of the Canadian Confederation, under the shelter of the British flag and British institutions?" Collections were made in Quebec for the "wounded of Ontario".

Because it was a provincial matter, Laurier was by no means eager to intervene in the Ontario school question, but he watched the campaign in Quebec with rising anxiety. He was persuaded that the "violent agitation stirred up by our Nationalist friends, instead of aiding in solution only makes the situation worse"; yet he was opposed to the restrictive nature of Regulation 17. What he wanted was a return to Mowat's policy of toleration; he believed that "every French child should receive an English education in the schools of Ontario, with a privilege of being also taught in French." He tried very hard to get the provincial Liberals of Ontario to work for some concession that would conciliate French Canadians, but without success, for the people of Ontario were deeply wounded by the French Nationalists' charges of Prussianism.

In the spring of 1916 the Quebec Liberal, Ernest Lapointe, introduced a resolution in the House of Commons that, while recognizing "the principle of provincial rights and the necessity of every child being given a thorough English education, respectfully suggests to the Legislative Assembly of Ontario the wisdom of making it clear that the privilege of the children of French parentage of being taught in their mother tongue be not interfered with." On this motion Laurier spoke with great eloquence and deep feeling. He did not "invoke the cold letter of any positive law", nor did he deny Ontario's supreme right to regulate education within the province; and he thought it deplorable that "men of French origin who, when France is fighting the fight of heroism which stirs the blood of mankind, remain with their blood cold, who tell us: 'No, we will not lift a finger to assist Britain in defending the integrity of France, but we want our wrongs to be righted in Ontario.' " Whatever happened in Ontario, he thought French Canadians ought to "take part in the great struggle that is going on today in the land of their ancestors for the cause of freedom, and of the civilization of mankind." All the same, he attacked the motto of certain Toronto imperialists, "one language and one language only", which he thought alien to British institutions that were based on "freedom and respect for minorities". He appealed "to the sense of justice and fair play of the people of Ontario, and to their appreciation of British institutions." He agreed that every child in Ontario should "receive the benefit of an English education"; but, "when I ask that every child of my own race should receive an English education, will you refuse us the privilege of education also in the language of our mothers and fathers?"

In that hard spring of 1916 Laurier's appeal for generosity fell on stony ground. Laurier's own Liberal party was scarcely united on this issue. The situation plunged Laurier into the depths of hopelessness. "I have lived too long," he said. "I have outlived Liberalism." He stated his intention of resigning immediately. Appalled, the Ontario Liberals (all except one) rallied to his support and voted for the Lapointe resolution—they had not realized "the Old Man" felt so deeply about it. But the western Liberals voted against Laurier and the Lapointe resolution and it was defeated. This was a prelude to the much greater disaster of conscription which, in the short run, broke the Liberal party and so nearly destroyed national unity—the cause closest to Laurier's heart—that Canada has scarcely yet recovered.

The war in Europe went badly for the allied countries in 1916; it went even worse in 1917. In that year the Russian revolution began to destroy Russia's military power on the eastern front and allowed Germany to concentrate her efforts on the western front, where a French offensive failed disastrously in the spring and all summer long the British suffered terrible losses. Among the casualties were a great many Canadians—20,000 in April and May 1917. Enlistments in Canada fell off sharply: in those same months there were only 3,000 recruits.

Prime Minister Borden, who was in London in the spring of 1917, knew how urgently the allied powers needed more troops. He knew that, as things stood, Canada's efforts fell short of those of Australia, New Zealand, and South Africa, and far, far short of Britain and France; he knew also that

Canada's contribution would not even be maintained at its present level if more recruits were not found. Borden and the Conservative government therefore decided to introduce conscription for a number of honourable reasons: to help win a just war, to honour obligations to the allied powers, to keep faith with the Canadian soldiers in Europe. Borden said in the House of Commons: "If what are left of 400,000 such men come back to Canada with fierce resentment in their hearts, conscious that they have been deserted and betrayed, how shall we meet them when they ask the reason? I am not so much concerned for the day when this Bill becomes law, as for the day when these men return if it is rejected." Borden's right-hand man in the cabinet, Arthur Meighen, believed "The war is paramount and transcends everything else." And he was not alone. J.W. Dafoe, Liberal editor of the Winnipeg *Free Press,* who was about as much an imperialist as Henri Bourassa, felt that Canada was "in the war as a principal which involved literally the sacrifice, if necessary, of the last man and the last dollar." The real reason that Canada was allied with Great Britain was that both were fighting for "freedom and democracy", a cause worthy of all support. In the black year of 1917 that seemed to mean conscription.

Not to Laurier, however. He was instinctively opposed to coercion all through his life, and his deep admiration for Great Britain was based on his belief that the British stood for individual freedom and tolerance. This nineteenth-century Britain was rapidly passing away during the First World War when individual liberty yielded to collective action, voluntary recruiting to conscription. But Laurier did not change. Unlike Borden he did not visit the front in Europe, nor did he visit the wounded Canadian soldiers in hospital in Britain—he had little direct contact with the war. However, he knew his Canada, and in particular he knew Quebec as Borden and the Conservative cabinet never would. To Laurier it was Canada, not the war, that was paramount and that transcended everything else: national unity came first, not the allied cause, however just. The front he knew best was Quebec, and Quebec he knew to be unalterably opposed to conscription.

Ever since the turn of the century Bourassa and the Nationalists had warned French Canadians that Canadian involvement in Britain's imperialist wars would lead straight to conscription in Canada. Laurier had constantly denied this charge—in the Drummond-Arthabaska by-election of 1910, during the election of 1911, and repeatedly in his recruiting speeches after 1914. The Nationalists did not believe him: they thought him weak, always ready to yield to imperialist pressures. By 1916 Bourassa was prepared to go further: it was Laurier himself, right from the time of the South African war, who had been leading French Canadians to conscription. He ended his attack with a bitter outburst: "Sir Wilfrid Laurier is the most nefarious man in the province of Quebec, in the whole of Canada!"

In 1917 the "monster of conscription," which Laurier had called a myth, came to life. Laurier, an honourable man, felt he had no alternative but to fight it. He refused Borden's invitation to join a Union government to implement conscription and explained his position carefully to the Ontario conscriptionist Liberal N.W. Rowell. For years and years he had protested to French Canadians that he was opposed to conscription. "Now if I were to waver, to hesitate or to flinch, I would simply hand over the province of Quebec to the extremists. I would lose the respect of the people whom I thus addressed and would deserve it. I would not only lose their respect but my own self-respect also." He did offer to support conscription if it were first presented to the Canadian people in a referendum and accepted by them; but this was a compromise that won little attention and no support.

Dafoe thought that fundamentally Laurier opposed conscription because he feared to lose to Bourassa "his proud position as the first and greatest of French Canadians". This is doubtful. Bourassa and Laurier belonged to quite different traditions. Like his grandfather before him, Bourassa was the champion of his people, their warm advocate. Laurier was not this kind of hero; he was never a Papineau, a Mercier, or a Bourassa. He was more like LaFontaine and Cartier a Canadian statesman whose great political object was the conciliation of English- and French-speaking Canadians. In 1917 his life's work was everywhere in danger, but nowhere more clearly than in Quebec, consumed by hatred of conscription. Laurier was certainly frightened of Bourassa—not because Bourassa threatened to eclipse him in Quebec, however, but because a Nationalist triumph would threaten the unity, perhaps the existence, of Canada. Conscription had to be opposed: "After the agitation which has been carried on upon this subject, if we were to hesitate at this moment, we would hand over the province to the extremists; in place of promoting national unity, it would open up a breach, perhaps fatal."

The course of Laurier and the Quebec Liberals was clear enough; that of the English-speaking Liberals was much more tortured. All through Canada there was an immense fondness for Laurier—no Canadian politician has since equalled his appeal—and nowhere was the affection more intense than within the Liberal party. In 1917 English-speaking Liberals who believed in Laurier and in conscription were miserably torn in their loyalties; they did not find it easy to leave Laurier and join Borden's Union government in the early fall of 1917. And Laurier felt wretched when they left. "Yesterday it was Pardee, and today it will be Graham! Graham and Pardee, as dear to me as my own brothers! Do not, however, think hard of them, for I do not. They have behaved all through most honourably, and there is not and there will not be any loss of friendship between us. The pain is not less acute on their side than on mine, and I know only too well the difficulties which faced them." The loss that hurt most was Fielding, his close political associate since 1896, the man he wanted to succeed him as leader of the Liberal party. The night he heard that Fielding had declared his support of the Union government, Laurier marked these verses from Psalm 55 in his Bible:

For it was not an enemy that reproached me; then I could have borne it; neither was it he that hated me that did magnify himself against me; then I would have hid myself from him.

But it was thou, a man mine equal, my guide, and mine acquaintance.

But not all of Laurier's colleagues abandoned him for the new Union government; and none declared their loyalty more movingly than Sir Allan Aylesworth, leader of the federal Ontario Liberals, who wrote: "Whither thou goest, I will go."

Only the remnants of the once-powerful Liberal party in the West and Ontario and the Maritimes remained to fight with Laurier his last federal election in December of 1917. He appeared undismayed, even invigorated, determined as he was to "face a murderous winter election, even if I have to die for it". For a seventy-six-year-old man in delicate health, that was a possibility, but Laurier campaigned energetically and courageously. The handicaps were hopelessly severe. Not only had he lost much of his party, but a good many Liberal voters had been disfranchised by the Wartime Elections Act, passed late in the summer of 1917, by which all those of "enemy birth or language" were denied a vote. Some of these were prairie Liberals—"Sifton's pets", they had once been called, but they were no longer. Sifton had promoted their immigration. Now, as an architect of the Union government, he accepted their disfranchisement. In addition, the Wartime Elections Act enfranchised all female relatives of soldiers overseas, a group pretty certain to favour the vigorous prosecution of the war, to support conscription and the Union government. Laurier doubted that conscription was overwhelmingly supported even in the English-speaking provinces, and it seemed that the Union government shared his belief, for just before the election it went further to make victory certain: farmers were assured that their sons would not be conscripted.

The election campaign was savage, particularly in the press. The Laurier Liberals had nothing to fear from *Le Devoir,* for Bourassa supported them as the lesser evil; but this newspaper's tempered praise was more than offset by abuse in the English-language press. J.S. Willison was now describing Laurier in his paper, the Toronto *News,* as "a demagogue, a charlatan and a mountebank". The Toronto *Mail and Empire* assured its readers that Laurier was the choice of the Kaiser. Perhaps ordinary people were less ferocious: certainly they still gave Laurier a hearing. In below-zero temperatures in Winnipeg thousands came to hear him speak and their cheers were deafening. It was the same everywhere he went in the West, but those cheers were not transformed into votes on election day. The Liberals won only 2 seats in the whole of western Canada, 8 in Ontario and 10 in the Maritimes; in Quebec they won 62 of the 65 seats. The government— Conservatives and Union Liberals—had a majority of 71 seats. Its members were determined to give all possible support to winning the war; they were indifferent, for the time being, to the hostility of Quebec.

After the elections of 1917 Laurier retained the appearance of tranquillity he had always shown to the public. Privately he nourished anxieties: "The racial chasm which is now opening at our feet may perhaps not be overcome for many generations," he had written to a friend a few weeks before the election. Later he regained more of his composure: "I still have faith in the sound sense of the Canadian people and in the broad forces that make for national unity on a basis of fair and respecting partnership. Once the war is over, no election, no dozen elections, no unscrupulous propaganda, can prevent Canadians more and more becoming Canadians first, and when they are so, we shall hear less and less of Ontario and of Quebec."

He continued to think that "when the war is over . . . it will be difficult to undo the mischief which has been done", but all the same he was ready to try. He had the capacity of a stoic to rise above his anxieties. So he continued, in 1918, as leader of the Liberal party. Chubby Power, just beginning his parliamentary career as Liberal M.P. for Quebec West, remembered Laurier in what was to be his last session. "He was always ready," Power wrote, "even anxious, to talk to any of his followers no matter how trivial the subject. One of the things that endeared him to the younger members of the party was his habit of meeting us in the corridors, inviting us into his office to smoke a cigarette, and passing five or ten minutes in asking us how Bill Jones was in such and such a village, how so-and-so was and how he was getting along, and inquiring about our own studies and our interests. After ten minutes' talking we returned to the House ready and eager to do anything we could for the leader with whom we were in such perfect communion of heart and mind."

Despite his increasing years and failing health, he kept his ability to look hard at the world around him and see, with his acute politician's eye, what was up. This is what he thought in January 1918: "The new world will be based upon a wide sweeping of privileges and a nearer approach to social equality; in other words this means the advent of democracy. In my judgement the advent of democracy will be a blessing, though as [in] everything human not an unmixed blessing, but will bring to the masses of mankind a greater share of happiness than they have ever had before." At a meeting of Liberal strategists during the summer, he tried to kindle an interest in labour questions, a rather novel subject for the elderly group.

In May 1918 Wilfrid and Zoë Laurier celebrated their golden wedding anniversary—fifty years together, instead of the one or two that the worried bride of 1868 had expected with her frail husband. Replying to a letter of congratulation from the widow of Ernest Pacaud, Laurier wrote: "I have been happy in my domestic life, happy in my public life. Now that I have reached the summit, my thoughts go back in preference to those days of Arthabaska." He spent his last summer there. It was a peaceful one; he was often sick—his physical strength was failing steadily. On his way back to Ottawa he stopped briefly at L'Assomption, talking a little to the young students there, looking at the old stone building and for a moment touching it. Then he got in the waiting car and continued on to Ottawa.

The war ended in November 1918, a year earlier than anyone had dared to predict in 1917. Partly because of this, conscription under the Military Service Act did not contribute much to the winning of the war. To be sure, even though it was administered inefficiently, it did produce over a hundred thousand soldiers, but of these less than half actually went overseas. Opposition to conscription led to serious riots in Quebec; more serious perhaps were the dark lingering memories of being oppressed by an English-speaking Canada. Ontario farmers were enraged when exemptions for their sons were cancelled in the spring of 1918, and organized labour—what there was of it—was sharply opposed to conscription. Outside of Quebec there were no riots, but after the war there was a full-scale political revolt by farmers and labour men against the old politicians who had been so willing to conscript manpower, so much less willing to conscript wealth by taxation.

Laurier's main preoccupation for the remaining few months of his life was re-uniting and rehabilitating the Liberal party. He made the way easy for the return of Fielding and George Graham and other conscriptionist Liberals. Even though Laurier disagreed with them, he understood why they had been conscriptionists; and he believed that the past should not be allowed to destroy the future. In his last speech he urged this point: "Let us forget the past and be again well-united Liberals, each acting only under the promptings of his conscience." The work of reconstruction was not complete by the time Laurier died, and his own spirit of reconciliation did not altogether prevail in the Liberal party. All the same he left a party in which French and English were still united, largely because of the influence of his strong and tolerant personality. On Mackenzie King, who became leader of the Liberal party after Laurier's death, he left an indelible impression of the importance of maintaining national unity. King totally lacked Laurier's charm, but he was quite capable of getting hold of Laurier's first principle and sticking to it. It may be argued that King and the Liberal party and all Canada thereby benefited.

But the force of Laurier's personality was felt well beyond the Liberal party; he reached right into the hearts of all Canadians, who have never since responded so unanimously to any politician. Ordinary people liked Laurier not because he was ordinary, for he was not—his manner was aristocratic, his dress elegant—but because he was so responsive. He liked his fellow Canadians, listened to them, reasoned with them. He did not always carry conviction: as he said, they cheered him but did not vote for him. All the same, those cheers meant something: they expressed the intense admiration Laurier always aroused, partly by his sheer intellectual abilities, partly because he always did his audiences the honour of appealing to their reason. He combined candour and charm in so irresistible a way that he managed to say what he wanted even to hostile audiences and individuals.

Laurier claimed early that he was an English liberal. This was never a simple vote-catching device. Nineteenth-century English liberalism stressed matters close to his heart: he believed in individual liberty and tolerance for minorities both instinctively and intellectually. These doctrines seemed terribly important to him in the Quebec of the 1870s when the ultramontanes, to whom tolerance was a vice, were working to eradicate the Liberal party; they seemed important still, especially around the turn of the century, when a sense of mission made so many English-speaking Canadians intolerably arrogant. Laurier thought Gladstone the greatest states-

The funeral of Sir Wilfrid Laurier, 20 February 1919

man of the nineteenth century, and what he liked best in
Gladstone was the tremendous energy he brought to bear
against "injustice, wrong, oppression". Laurier himself did
not have Gladstone's crusading zeal: he was temperamentally
much more like another statesman he admired, Abraham
Lincoln. In many ways Canada resembled the United States:
both were large new countries filled with mixtures of peoples
not used to each other, all too often simultaneously frightened of being dominated and struggling to dominate. In a
deeply united and tolerant Great Britain a great statesman
could safely crusade a little. In North America, where there
were dozens of crusaders, great statesmen endeavoured to
stifle their enthusiasm and work for reconciliation.

All the same, Laurier had a very unAmerican disbelief in
the "melting pot" theory of nationality. His preference for
British traditions and his French-Canadian origin strengthened his feeling that Canadian nationality could flourish even
though Canada was made up of a variety of minority groups.
He thought English, French, Scottish, Irish, and others could
all survive and Canada would still be strong, just like a Gothic
cathedral—"a harmonious whole, in which granite, marble,
oak and other materials were blended. This cathedral is the
image of the nation that I hope to see Canada become. As
long as I live, as long as I have the power to labour in the
service of my country, I shall repel the idea of changing the
nature of its different elements. I want the marble to remain
the marble; I want the granite to remain the granite; I want
the oak to remain the oak."

Among French Canadians Laurier's prestige has perhaps
dwindled since his death, for many intellectuals in Quebec
have tended to be more interested in French-Canadian than
Canadian nationalism. While Laurier lived, however, most

French Canadians admired him enormously. His was a great success story, and his fellow citizens savoured all his triumphs from the Jubilee celebrations on. It was years before Bourassa had any success in rousing the feeling that Laurier was betraying French-Canadian interests. And after 1896 Laurier never lost the votes of the majority of French Canadians to the Liberal party.

Laurier died on Monday, February 17, 1919, just before the opening of a new session of parliament. There was no long agony for him. The Saturday before, after attending a Canadian Club luncheon, he suffered his first stroke at his office in the Victoria Museum. Disliking fuss, he did not call the chauffeur but took a streetcar home. The next day there was a second stroke, then hours of unconsciousness. He recovered enough at one point to murmur to his wife: "C'est fini."

There were thousands of mourners and thousands of messages of condolence. One person who called at the house on Laurier Avenue to pay his respects was Arthur Meighen, author of the Military Service Act and the Wartime Elections Act. He took his nine-year-old daughter with him. "You're too young to understand", he told her, "but I want you to be able to say that you saw one of the finest men I have ever known."

Sources and Further Reading

Paperback editions are marked with an asterisk (*).

There is a wealth of material on Laurier and his period in his own letters and speeches, in reminiscences by his contemporaries, and in scholarly studies by historians and journalists of his own time and ours. In some respects the best place to begin is O.D. Skelton's *Life and Letters of Sir Wilfrid Laurier* (2 vols, Toronto, 1921; abridged in the Carleton Library, 2 vols, Toronto, 1965). Skelton had the benefit of long discussions with Laurier on various aspects of his career and was the first to use his papers, which are now in the Public Archives of Canada. His biography is strengthened by the inclusion of long quotations from Laurier's speeches and writings, though it is a trifle dated in its emphasis on Laurier's struggle to defeat the British imperialists. Skelton's admiration of Laurier is profound and uncritical; J.W. Dafoe's series of review articles, published in 1922 as *Laurier: A Study in Canadian Politics* (Carleton Library, Toronto, 1963), is a wholesome antidote. A recent biography by Joseph Schull, *Laurier: The First Canadian* (Toronto, 1965), is extremely readable. Schull has a strong sense of atmosphere and character and establishes the French-Canadian setting particularly well; this perhaps compensates for a certain lack of clarity in organization. H. Blair Neatby's doctoral thesis, "Laurier and a Liberal Quebec" (University of Toronto, 1956), is an admirably clear and careful piece of work. Robert Rumilly's *Sir Wilfrid Laurier, Canadian* (Paris, 1931) is short but useful as far as it goes.

Two biographies written by friends of Laurier are rewarding. The first is J.S. Willison, *Sir Wilfrid Laurier and the Liberal Party* (2 vols, Toronto, 1903); less majestic, but not to be overlooked, is L.-O. David's little book, *Laurier et son temps* (Montreal, 1905).

Among other materials directly relating to Laurier, the following should be singled out. *Wilfrid Laurier on the Platform, 1871-1890* (Quebec, 1890) is a useful translation of Laurier's early speeches edited by Ulric Barthe. F.H. Underhill explores the relations between Laurier and Blake, with generous reference to their letters, in "Laurier and Blake, 1882-1891" and "Laurier and Blake, 1891-2", in the *Canadian Historical Review* (hereafter abbreviated as *CHR*), December 1939 and June 1943 respectively. Other more personal letters are published in Lucien Pacaud, *Sir Wilfrid Laurier—Letters to My Father and Mother*

(Toronto, 1935). Marc La Terreur deftly handles another of Laurier's friendships in his article "Correspondance Laurier—Mme Joseph Lavergne, 1891-1893" in the *Canadian Historical Association Annual Report* (hereafter abbreviated as *CHAAR*), 1964. Margaret Banks deals with "The Change in Liberal Party Leadership, 1887" (*CHR*, 1957) and Paul Stevens with "Laurier, Aylesworth, and the Decline of the Liberal Party in Ontario" (*CHAAR*, 1968).

Reminiscences by political contemporaries of Laurier very often provide useful insights. This is particularly true of Armand Lavergne, *Trente ans de vie nationale* (Montreal, 1934); Charles Langelier, *Souvenirs politiques de 1878-1900* (2 vols. Quebec 1909); and P.A. Choquette, *Un Demi-Siècle de vie politique* (Montreal, 1936). Among English-speaking Canadians, Sir John Willison's *Reminiscences: Political and Personal* (Toronto, 1919) are the most acute and interesting. There is also material in the following: Sir Richard Cartwright, *Reminiscences* (Toronto, 1912); G.W. Ross, *Getting into Parliament and After* (Toronto, 1913); Maurice Pope (ed.), *Public Servant: The Memoirs of Sir Joseph Pope* (Toronto, 1960); Henry Borden (ed.), **Robert Laird Borden: His Memoirs* (2 vols, Toronto, 1938; Carleton Library, Toronto, 1969); and Norman Ward (ed.), *A Party Politician: The Memoirs of Chubby Power* (Toronto, 1966).

Edward Blake and Henri Bourassa, two political figures who were of immense importance to Laurier, are also important to students of his career. F.H. Underhill's essays on Blake are all worth reading: his "Edward Blake" in C.T. Bissell (ed.), **Our Living Tradition* (Toronto, 1957) makes a good beginning. On Henri Bourassa, who has received much more attention from historians, two items may be singled out: a judicious article by M.P. O'Connell, "The Ideas of Henri Bourassa", in the *Canadian Journal of Economics and Political Science* (August 1953), and L.-O. David's perceptive sketch in *Souvenirs et biographies, 1870-1910* (Montreal, 1911). David illuminates everyone he describes.

Visitors often made acute observations about the Canada of Laurier's time, but no one was so lynx-eyed as André Siegfried, whose first book on Canada, **The Race Question in Canada* (Paris, 1906; Carleton Library, Toronto, 1966) remains a penetrating study. Understandably less profound but deeply interesting is *The Canadian Journal of Lady Aberdeen, 1893-1898* (Toronto, 1960), edited with an excellent introduction by John T. Saywell. J.A. Hobson, *Canada Today*

(London, 1906) and Rupert Brooke, *Letters from America* (New York, 1916) are also worth reading.

For Laurier's French-Canadian background, the best place to start is Mason Wade, *The French Canadians, 1760-1945* (Toronto, 1955; revised paperback edition, 2 vols, 1968); for a closer look, see Robert Rumilly's multi-volumed *Histoire de la province de Québec* (Montreal, various dates). Further material is found in the following articles: Barbara Fraser, "The Political Career of Sir Hector Langevin" (*CHR*, June 1961); Laurier LaPierre, "Joseph Israel Tarte and the McGreevy-Langevin Scandal" (*CHAAR*, 1961); H. Blair Neatby and John Saywell, "Chapleau and the Conservative Party in Quebec" (*CHR*, March 1956); and P. Sylvain, "Liberalisme et ultramontanisme au Canada français . . ." in W.L. Morton (ed.), *The Shield of Achilles* (Toronto, 1968).

The following books on political contemporaries, some of them closely connected with Laurier, are also important: D.G. Creighton, *John A. Macdonald* (2 vols, Toronto, 1952, 1955); J.W. Dafoe, *Clifford Sifton in Relation to his Times* (Toronto, 1931); R.M. Dawson, *William Lyon Mackenzie King, 1874-1923* (Toronto, 1958): Andrée Desilets, *Hector-Louis Langevin* (Québec, 1969); H.S. Ferns and B. Ostry, *The Age of Mackenzie King: The Rise of the Leader* (London, 1955); Roger Graham, *Arthur Meighen*, Vol. 1 (Toronto, 1960); and D.C. Thomson, *Alexander Mackenzie: Clear Grit* (Toronto, 1960).

Other useful books and articles on various problems and changes in Canada during Laurier's lifetime include the following: G.F.G. Stanley, *Louis Riel* (Toronto, 1963); Lovell Clark (ed.), *The Manitoba School Question: Majority Rule or Minority Rights?* (Toronto, 1968); Craig Brown (ed.), *Minorities, Schools and Politics* (Toronto, 1969); F.A. Walker, *Catholic Education and Politics in Ontario* (Toronto, 1964); G.R. Stevens, *Canadian National Railways*, Vol. 2 (Toronto, 1962); D.C. Masters, *Reciprocity, 1846-1911* (Ottawa, 1961); Max Beloff, *Imperial Sunset, Vol. 1: Britain's Liberal Empire, 1897-1921* (London, 1969); Carl Berger (ed.), *Imperial Relations in the Age of Laurier* (Toronto, 1969); A.R.M. Lower, *Canadians in the Making* (Toronto, 1958); A.P. Thornton, *The Imperial Idea and Its Enemies* (London, 1959); F.H. Underhill, *The Image of Confederation* (Toronto, 1963); and Carl Berger (ed.), *Conscription 1917* (Toronto, n.d.). P.B. Waite's *Canada 1874-1896: Arduous Destiny* (Toronto, 1971) is both scholarly and readable—a delight, in fact.

Index